Magnificent Strangers

Ann Wedgeworth

Radiant BOOKS
Gospel Publishing House/Springfield, Mo. 65802

02-0568

MAGNIFICENT STRANGERS

Library of Congress Catalog Card Number 78-67446
ISBN 0-88243-568-X
Printed in the United States of America

Dedicated to My Husband,
William W. Wedgeworth,
Who Made This Book Possible

Foreword

Audrey Mieir, Evie Tornquist, Ralph Wilkerson, Billy Graham, Betty Malz, Norma Zimmer, Dr. V. Raymond Edman, and Corrie ten Boom. . . . What do all of these well-known personalities have in common?

Each has a story to tell of a modern-day angelic visitation.

Audrey Mieir, the beloved composer, while on national television said she often hears the flutter of angels' wings. In her book *Audrey Mieir–The Laughter and the Tears* she tells the following story of a reenactment of the Nativity:

> Father, I thank You. I praise You for allowing me to give the world "His Name Is Wonderful." You sang it to me that Christmas morning in our little church in Duarte, California. The manger scene was very humble: Mary was a teenager . . . baby Jesus was a doll . . . the angel's halo was crooked . . . the blue jeans of the wise men showed beneath their dads' old bathrobes. The fragrance of pine boughs filled the air. The children's faces were filled with wonder as they watched the familiar scene being reenacted. Old people wiped away tears, remembering other Christmases long gone.
>
> Suddenly, the rustle of angels' wings filled the air. . . . And then Dr. Luther Mieir, my beloved brother-in-law and pastor of the church, lifted his voice

> and his hands and said, "His name is wonderful, Jesus my Lord!"
>
> Thank You, Father, for that moment out of time. You wanted the world to praise Your Son, not just as a baby in a manger, but as God in human flesh. So You sang it to me with the angels standing by, and I wrote it in the back of my Bible, just as I heard it. . . .[1]

Evie Tornquist's anointed singing has blessed the hearts of thousands in Billy Graham's crusades and on national television. In an interview on the *700 Club,* Evie told how she saw guardian angels around her home one night when she was frightened and alone.

Ralph Wilkerson is the author of the best-selling book *Beyond and Back,* the pastor and founder of Melodyland Congregation, and the chancellor of the Melodyland School of Theology. He relates how an angel spent the night with his father-in-law, R. A. Work, who was deathly ill in the hospital. Later angels escorted him to the gate of heaven, but were compelled to send him back to earth in answer to his wife's prayers.[2]

Billy Graham also describes modern-day angelic visitations in his book *Angels: God's Secret Agents.*[3] And Betty Malz vividly recalls her journey to heaven with an angel escort in her book *My Glimpse of Eternity.*[4]

Norma Zimmer, star of the popular *Lawrence Welk Show* for over 18 years, was visited by an angel when her son was very ill:

> Suddenly I noticed a brightness behind me. I looked around. Standing near the bed was a lovely young blonde woman with a white blouse and a dark skirt. I was stunned! I was not sleeping—in fact, I was very

> wide awake. Transfixed, I watched her for what seemed like thirty seconds. She just stood there with a radiant smile on her face, looking down at Ron. Then she faded away. It was a glorious experience. I felt no fear—just awe. I have always believed that I was permitted to see Ron's guardian angel.[5]

God's love and presence surround us. He has sent His powerful, magnificent messengers to many individuals. The electrifying presence of these heavenly beings has comforted hearts, calmed fears, and recharged the faith of people everywhere. Their stories are written throughout the pages of this book.

Contents

CHAPTER ONE

Messengers of God

"Be not forgetful to entertain strangers: for thereby some have entertained angels unawares."
Hebrews 13:2

Some years ago a small girl strayed into the street, and a large heavy truck ran over her. The driver stopped when he realized what had happened, and the mother was called as a crowd gathered around the scene of the accident. The distraught mother was told the back dual tires of the truck had run over her daughter. But, when she reached the girl, she was amazed her daughter was not dead. In fact, she was not injured at all!

Amid exclamations of relief, the child stood up and said, "But didn't you see that angel? I saw him take his hand and lift up the wheels as they went over me! So, I didn't even feel the tires!"[1]

This true story was related by Gladys Wolverton, a missionary to South Africa, who had read the story in a newspaper article. Mrs. Wolverton also told the following astonishing story:

For several days before a 10-year-old girl's death, an angel came to visit her in the hospital. As her mother sat by her bedside, the girl described the angel's presence and beauty.

The little girl had contracted chicken pox and complications had followed. Her heart had been damaged and she was seriously ill. The mother was very bitter at the thought of losing her only daughter. Even though the mother could not see the angel, "she knew when he was there because of her daughter's behavior and descriptions of his amazing beauty." The mother tried everything possible "to discourage the angel's visits and to persuade her daughter that the visitations were not real."

One day the young girl stretched out her arms and said to her mother, "This time he has come to take me! Please don't try to hold me back. I must go!" In a moment she was gone.[2]

Mrs. Wolverton added that she was acquainted with the Christian nurse who had taken care of the little girl before her death.

To witness the presence of a majestic being—an angel—is to have the privilege of glimpsing a little of the glory and splendor of heaven. There are many people today around the world who have seen these magnificent strangers. Modern-day stories of such beautiful, unusual encounters have been reported by ministers, missionaries, and workers of various denominations. Testimony of their presence abounds everywhere.

Evidence of their existence also goes back to the very beginning. Angels are mentioned hundreds of times in the Scriptures. They came as messengers of God, appearing to the everyday people of Abraham's day and the great prophets of the Old Testament. Magnificent celestial beings brought the joyous message of Christ's birth. They ministered to Him in

His death and announced to the world His resurrection.

Angels stood by at the ascension of Christ and ministered on numerous occasions to the apostles and other believers, performing miracles on their behalf. Their ministry did not end there but continues today, as witnessed by Mrs. Hanson, a missionary to Africa.

Rev. and Mrs. Hanson pastored a church in Durban, South Africa. Mrs. Hanson traveled home to Norway during the war, only to find that war regulations prevented her from returning to her family on the mission field. Norway had been invaded by the Nazi Regime. All were prohibited from having worship of any kind. Being sent to a concentration camp was the penalty for possessing a radio. Mrs. Hanson stayed with her sister, living with the constant knowledge that their home could be searched any time of the day or night by Hitler's gestapo.

One night Mrs. Hanson awoke suddenly, alerted by a strange sound coming from the other room. She stared intently into the darkness. From where she was, she could see through the night shadows into the living room. Gradually, she became aware of the form of a man standing there and realized he was reading from the 91st Psalm:

> He that dwelleth in the secret place of the Most High shall abide under the shadow of the Almighty. I will say of the Lord, He is my refuge and my fortress: my God; in him will I trust. . . . *Thou shalt not be afraid* for the terror by night; nor for the arrow that flieth by day. . . . A thousand shall fall at thy side, and ten thousand at thy right hand; but it shall not come nigh thee. . . .
>
> *There shall no evil befall thee,* neither shall any plague come nigh thy dwelling. For *he shall give his*

angels charge over thee, to keep thee in all thy ways. *They shall bear thee up in their hands,* lest thou dash thy foot against a stone (Psalm 91:1, 2, 5, 7, 10-12).

He finished reading and then just disappeared! Mrs. Hanson became aware of an overwhelming sense of courage and the presence of God. She and her sister were inspired and encouraged by this incident and, as a result, began to bicycle to various parts of Norway to help spread the gospel message.[3]

What would it be like to witness the presence of an angel? Another witness, a little girl in South Africa, knows the answer to that question. Her story is told by Miss Wanda Moore, missionary to the Congo.[4]

"I was a missionary in the Congo (now called Zaire) in that vast area of the Ituri Forest. Many people there can neither read nor write, and it always amazed me how God led and spoke to his dear Christians by dreams, visions, angels, and 'that still small voice.' I learned of several experiences of angels watching over people, especially children, protecting them from snakes, dangers, and leading them through the dense forest when they did not know the way."

One of the experiences Miss Moore relates was of a young girl who became very ill with malaria and early one morning died. The custom there is that they must be buried the same day, due to heavy tropical heat. So, the family began the necessary arrangement to bury her in the late afternoon.

As the time for the funeral drew near, they began the procession to the burial place and, upon reaching the grave site, laid her body on a mat beside the open grave. The graveside service was conducted, and just as it was time for the body to be lowered into the grave, she suddenly sat up and said, "Where am I?"

Then to everyone's amazement, she began to tell them what had happened to her that day. That morning an angel had appeared to her, saying she had come to take her to heaven. The little girl told how she had seen the great beauty of heaven and Jesus, Mary, and many others.

The angel took the little girl to see her brother, whom she had never seen before. In fact, she did not even know she had a brother in heaven. Belonging to a large family, she was unaware that her parents had lost one of their first children, who had died as a small child. She had been born many years later and no one had told her about her brother. She also met other relatives who had died before she was born, including her grandparents.

She told of the great beauty of heaven, the happiness there, and how she wanted to stay there. However, the angel told her she "must return to her family, relatives, and the people of her village, as so many of them were not saved, and she was to tell them so they could get right with God."

Imagine the impact of her words on all who heard her story. They were amazed as she told them the names of the people she had seen in heaven, some of whom she had never known. Many who heard her story "fell on their knees and cried out to God and were saved."

Miss Moore writes: "For several weeks to follow she was brought to the churches of this district to tell her story at their Sunday services. Crowds flocked to hear her and many were saved each week."

The above events took place in modern times; however, each one could be compared with a similar angelic appearance in God's Word. A favorite Scripture passage that is often quoted is Psalm 34:7: "The angel of the Lord encampeth round about them that fear him, and delivereth them."

An example of a scriptural angelic appearance occurred when Paul was shipwrecked: "For there stood by me this night the angel of God . . ." (Acts 27:23). God still sends His heavenly escorts today to encourage and commission His people, just as the angel was sent to Gideon to tell him of the exciting part he was to have in delivering the Israelites from their enemies (Judges 6:12).

Another example from the Bible is found in the story of the beggar Lazarus. Jesus said when Lazarus died he "was carried by the angels" into heaven (Luke 16:22). Revelation 1:1 reveals that an angel was sent to show John heaven. God is able also to extend this great privilege to another of His sons or daughters, such as the little girl in Africa, for He has said in His Word: "Except ye be converted, and become as little children, ye shall not enter into the kingdom of heaven" (Matthew 18:3). All we need is that childlike faith and trust in Him to enter into all heaven's glory.

If an angel delivered Daniel from the lions' den (Daniel 6:22), how much more would our Heavenly Father's love be extended to send His angel to protect a small child from the wheels of a truck!

Romans 8:14 tells us: "As many as are led by the Spirit of God, they are the sons of God." And verse 16 says: "The Spirit itself beareth witness with our spirit, that we are the children of God." Therefore, we know He will protect, encourage, and correct us as a father does his own family.

There are many ministries of the angels of God, and the multitude of reports from all over the world give us a glimpse into their activities in carrying out the will of God.

Dr. V. Raymond Edman, former president and chancellor of Wheaton College, had the following experience while serving as a missionary:

> It was . . . at Riobamba that Edman believed he had a heavenly visitant. Their home was surrounded by a protective fence, iron grillwork, and a locked gate. He heard the bell ring one day in the spring of 1925 and hurried to the gate. An unusually attractive Indian woman was there and spoke to him in commendation of his work and assured him of God's blessing upon it.
>
> She left, and when he quickly went out to catch her so that he could invite her to stay with them, she was nowhere to be seen. He could see the only way she could have gone in any direction, and there was no side street or building she could have entered. He concluded an angel had visited him, as stated in Hebrews 13:2. He often told this story and used it in periodicals and in one of his books.[5]

Another author and speaker of world renown, Corrie ten Boom, relates a story in her book *Marching Orders for the End Battle.* This event took place in the Congo at a time when there were many uprisings from the rebels:

> When the rebels advanced on a school where two hundred children of missionaries lived, they planned to kill both children and teachers. In the school they knew of the danger and therefore went to prayer. Their only protection was a fence and a couple of soldiers, while the enemy, who came closer and closer, amounted to sev-

eral hundreds. When the rebels were close by, suddenly something happened: they turned around and ran away! The next day the same thing happened and again on the third day.

One of the rebels was wounded and was brought to the mission hospital. When the doctor was busy dressing his wounds, he asked him: "Why did you not break into the school as you planned?"

"We could not do it. We saw hundreds of soldiers in white uniforms and we became scared."

In Africa soldiers never wear white uniforms, so it must have been angels. What a wonderful thing that the Lord can open the eyes of the enemy so that they see angels! We have the Bible and faith, and by faith we see invisible things.[6]

A similar report of angelic protection came from a medical missionary:

Angel Guard

"A medical missionary and his companion had to walk some distance to collect a sum of money which had been sent to a bank on their account. Night overtook them before they could reach home: so, committing themselves to God, they lay down to sleep on the lonely hillside and finished their journey the next morning.

"Some weeks later a man who came to the hospital for treatment stared at the missionary and said, 'I have seen you before.'

" 'No,' replied the missionary, 'I don't think we have met.'

" 'Oh, yes, we have!' said the man. 'You were sleeping on a hillside a few weeks ago. Several of us saw you at the bank and followed you, intending to rob you when it was dark, but we didn't dare because of the soldiers.'

" 'Soldiers?' The missionary laughed. 'There were no soldiers with us, my friend.'

"The bandit was adamant. 'Yes there were—we counted them. There were sixteen of them and they had swords.'

"The missionary humored the man and dismissed it as a hallucination. After telling the incident while on furlough, the missionary was approached by a friend who asked, 'What date was it when you camped on the hillside?' The missionary found the date in his diary and his questioner checked the date in his own appointment book.

" 'That night,' he said, 'we had our weekly prayer meeting. Your name was brought forward for prayer, and,' he added, 'there were sixteen of us in the meeting that night.' "[7]

And then there is the intriguing story of Elizabeta:

Katala Elume and his wife Elizabeta, pastors in the Republic of Zaire, felt called to open a work in a new area among the Zande tribe, a good many miles from where they had been working, and a few hundred miles from their own tribal area. At last the time came when a missionary was going through this area to which Elume felt called, and the missionary agreed to transport Elume and his family and few belongings to the village. Because of a delayed departure, they arrived at their destination very late in the evening. The missionary, unprepared for camping out, simply helped them to unload their belongings and, taking leave of them, drove on his way.

They were strangers among strangers, not knowing the area or the people at all. They sat among their belongings wondering what to do next. Night was approaching, no one had welcomed them, and the children were hungry. They had thought that perhaps the missionary would seek to make some contacts for them or even introduce them to the head of the village, though the missionary was not acquainted with the people either. But they had arrived late and the missionary was unable to stay.

They were feeling very discouraged when suddenly a woman approached Elizabeta and offered to go to the water hole to get them some water. Gratefully, Elizabeta found a water pot among her belongings. Encouraged by this show of friendliness, they began preparing supper, and soon someone came by and showed them a house where they could spend the night.

The next morning the villagers were more friendly. Not seeing the woman who had befriended them the evening before, Elume and Elizabeta inquired about her among the people, but the villagers insisted there was no woman in the neighborhood answering to her description, and none of them had seen this strange woman the evening before. In time, Elume and Elizabeta came to firmly believe the Lord had sent an angel to encourage them that first night in the village.

Some time later, Elume had to be gone for a few days. That night Elizabeta was frightened. Alone with her children in a strange land, she began to pray. "Lord, you know we are among strangers, among people of a different tribe, and no Christians are anywhere near. Will you protect me and the children and take away my fear?"

After Elizabeta had gone to bed, she heard the door open, scraping against the ground. A person with a sword in his hand came in and seated himself on the children's bed. Immediately she recognized him as an angel by his appearance, clothing, and the sword in his hand. She dropped off into an untroubled sleep, praising the Lord for His protection. The next morning at dawn, just as she was awakening, she heard the door open and close again as the angelic visitor took his departure. During the rest of her husband's absence, Elizabeta felt no fear. The angel's visit had reassured her that truly the Lord was watching over her.

Some months later the pastor was away again. During the night Elizabeta became very ill. Again she called upon God.

"Lord, here I am alone with these small children. If I die during my husband's absence, what will happen to the children?"

While she was praying, once again she heard the door open, and the *same angelic visitor* stepped into their mud house. He seated himself on her bed and, as he did so, she felt the healing touch of the Lord upon her and was able to drop off to sleep. The next morning when she awakened she did not see her visitor, but she was completely healed of her illness. Elizabeta and Elume spent many years in this village establishing a strong church.[8]

The beautiful story of Elizabeta and Elume was told by Assemblies of God missionary Gail Winters of the Republic of Zaire, a member of a Bible translation committee.

Each one of these reports is substantial evidence of the great love of God and His desire to move all the majestic powers of heaven to answer the cry of His people and meet their every need.

CHAPTER TWO

A Stranger Came

"And he lifted up his eyes and looked, and, lo, three men stood by him: and when he saw them, he ran to meet them from the tent door, and bowed himself toward the ground."

Genesis 18:2

The powers of heaven are unlimited. According to Landrum Leavell, "The Bible is unapologetically supernatural."[1] Angels possess qualities and powers unknown to man. C. Leslie Miller makes an interesting statement in his book *All About Angels:*

> Someone has suggested that angels are visible, but our eyes are not made to see them. Human sight is adjusted to only a small portion of the light waves and is far from being perfect or complete. Animals and birds see and hear things beyond our range of sight and hearing.[2]

What does an angel look like? The Bible seems to indicate an angel may appear in more than one form. For instance, sometimes an angel may materialize in brilliant array as at the resurrection of Christ. Other times he may look like a man, as indicated in the story of Abraham. Dr. Lewis Chafer in his book *Systematic Theology* states:

> The appearance of angels may be as occasion demands, so like man that they pass as men. How else could some "entertain angels unawares" (Heb. 13:2)? On the other hand, their appearance is sometimes in dazzling white and blazing glory (Matt. 28:24)[3]

This ability to look like men seems to explain why the Scriptures say that as Abraham stood in the tent door, he looked up and saw three "men" standing by him. Apparently, one of these "men" was the Lord himself. The other two were no doubt angels accompanying Him.

Clarke's Commentary says: "To Abraham these appeared at first as men; but he *entertained angels unawares*, see Heb. xiii. 2."[4]

The Lord had an extremely important message for Abraham, and He had chosen to tell it to Abraham himself. Abraham prepared a feast for his visitors. After they had eaten, the Lord told Abraham his wife Sarah would have a son, even though she had been barren all of her life and was now old (Genesis 18:1-15). This was to be the son through which the promised Messiah would come and all the nations of the world would be blessed.

As the Lord was leaving, He confided to Abraham His plan to visit Sodom and destroy it because of the evil there. As Abraham pleaded with the Lord for Sodom and his nephew Lot, who lived there, the two "men" started toward Sodom. Genesis 18:22 says: "And the *men* turned their faces from thence, and went toward Sodom: but Abraham stood yet before the Lord."

The first verse in the next chapter says, "There came two *angels* to Sodom at [evening] . . ." (19:1).

They came to rescue Lot and his wife and to destroy Sodom.

References to angels appearing as men occur many times in the Scriptures. The angel Gabriel visited Daniel: "Then, behold, there stood before me as the appearance of a man" (Daniel 8:15). At the ascension of Christ the Bible states: "Two men stood by . . . in white apparel" (Acts 1:10). The apostle Paul says there are celestial bodies and terrestrial bodies (1 Corinthians 15:40). Visiting celestial beings have been known to perform a variety of tasks, such as cooking meals for the prophet Elijah (1 Kings 19:5-8) and rolling away the stone at the tomb (Matthew 28:2).

The miraculous story of the stranger who helped Kaleen Ladd at the time of a car accident and then could never be found again is fascinating. Kaleen's husband, Jim Ladd, was attending Biola College at the time. Later he wrote the following story for a class while attending seminary in Portland.[5]

A Doctor or an Angel?

"Here it was only one week after the accident and yet we could not locate the doctor. He had treated my wife at the scene—he had saved her life, and yet it seemed that he simply did not exist.

"I had to ask myself, was this man really a doctor? If so, how could he have done what he did? If not, who was he or . . . what was he? What would you have done in that same situation? Would you have forgotten about it, or would you have investigated more? Let me tell you how it all started.

"It was September 1969, and we were living in

Whittier, California. I was attending Biola College and my wife, Kaleen was working as the secretary to the director of the Southern California Billy Graham Crusade in Anaheim.

"The morning of the first Sunday meeting we needed to be at the stadium to prepare some last minute details. We were very excited about these meetings as they were the result of long months of hard work and planning, so we quickly readied ourselves and left the house. After picking up a friend we proceeded on toward the stadium.

"We were traveling down a main street, when suddenly a car pulled right into our path. I only had time to just get my foot to the brake before we hit. I blacked-out momentarily because my next recollection was of looking over and seeing Kaleen covered with blood and gasping for breath. It seems that our friend who was sitting in the back seat was thrown forward into the back of Kaleen's seat causing it to break loose and throwing her into the windshield. We later learned that she had massive brain damage. But at that instant I only recognized she was seriously hurt.

"I again blacked-out. But the police record states that one of the witnesses to the accident was a doctor standing in front of a small community hospital across the street. He ran over and seeing Kaleen's condition, pulled her out of the car and performed a tracheotomy—that is he made an incision in Kaleen's throat so she could breathe.

"Now you might say that is all fine and good. Wasn't God good to have a doctor right at the scene? Yes, He was good. But He was more than good because that man was more than a doctor.

"You see, he performed a very complicated operation, a risky one at least. It is an operation which requires special instruments and great care to be taken. He did it with such skill and finesse that all the doctors and nurses who later worked on Kaleen remarked at the beauty of what is often an ugly scar. And he did all this in a matter of *two minutes!* It is a matter of record that the first police officer on the scene arrived two minutes after the accident and this 'doctor' was already finished.

"This 'doctor' stayed on the scene long enough to identify himself to the police and see Kaleen off in an ambulance and then was gone.

"Two days later I tried to find him at the little community hospital but they had never heard of him. Later I tried locating him through the California State Medical Registry, but with no results. As far as we could determine this man did not exist.

"If this man was a doctor how could he have done what is impossible medically? How did he get his instruments so quickly let alone do the operation in the street in so short a time and with such skill?

"But on the other hand if this 'man' was an angel all these questions are answered. With God 'nothing is impossible,' and as His representative for that situation, the angel merely used God's power to perform the surgery. And what is time to God? Could not He who exists eternally have enabled His angel to do in minutes that which takes a finite man much longer? And would not the all-knowing God equip His angel with the proper instruments with which to do that most skillful job?

"There is no doubt in our minds and hearts that God saw fit to save Kaleen's life by sending an angel to do what no human could ever have done at that point. Yet no matter how we see that incident, God was in it, doing the miraculous whether through man or angel. *Praise His name!*"

Kaleen's mother, Wanda Cummings (who, with her husband Ken, served many years as Conservative Baptist missionaries), adds a few interesting notes to Jim's story. She says when they arrived at the hospital, they were told Kaleen had a flat EEG, or a flat reading of the brain-wave test. The doctors said her condition was so serious she could not live or, if she did live, she would be a vegetable.

Ken and Wanda assured the neurosurgeon that Kaleen was in God's hands and anything God chose to do, whether He took her or caused her to remain, they would accept as the will of God for her life. They told him many people were praying for her and also for her doctors that the Lord would give them wisdom in undertaking for her. This neurosurgeon just shook his head and thanked them. The very next night he came to them again, after they had seen their daughter and the condition she was in, and said, "You know, your prayers must be doing some good."

They had thought perhaps the doctor who had operated on Kaleen had come from the small private hospital on the corner until Jim, Ken Cummings, and their son Kenny went to the hospital to thank the doctor. The receptionist, however, insisted they did not have a doctor by that name. In fact, they did not have any doctor on duty at all that morning, as it had been a Sunday morning when the accident occurred.

Kaleen and Jim later went to the police to try to find the doctor so they could thank him. They learned through the police that there was no one in the entire Los Angeles area by that name.

Some time later, Kaleen went back to the hospital for an examination. The neurosurgeon took her in to a room where there were many physicians, neurosurgeons, and specialists, and said, "Fellows, I want you to look at this girl! We know that she came in the hospital with a flat EEG, and we have taken many electro-encephalographs. The last one we took was perfectly normal. I want you to observe her. She is an unusual case, and we can't explain it medically."

Those who know Kaleen say she is a walking miracle. A miracle of God's grace, mercy, and protection.

The Unknown Friend

In another modern-day story, a man completely unknown to two Bible students intervened in their behalf. This exciting story of two students of the Middle East Evangelical Theological School (MEETS) was written by Carol Corpany and appeared in the *Middle East Outreach Reporter.*[6] She tells how one young man explained why he was finally able to get permission to leave his country to study at MEETS. "God sent an angel to go into that office before me," he said.

The law of that country would not allow him to leave his country to study at MEETS. As a final effort he had gone to the proper office to make his request anyhow. There he was told that "a very important person" had been there "immediately before him and had told the officials to give him and another young man permission to leave the country."

These two young students are of humble backgrounds and knew no "important person." The Lord had sent an angel to conduct this matter of business!

How great is God's love! Greater than the mind of man can comprehend! Paul says: "O the depth of the riches both of the wisdom and knowledge of God! how unsearchable are his judgments, and his ways past finding out!" (Romans 11:33).

Apart from a miracle of God, it is impossible to explain the following incredible story told by Gladys Behnke Triplett.[7]

Thirteen at the Table

"The plainly dressed woman who rang the doorbell at our home in Newberg, Oregon, about 10:30 one morning, was a complete stranger to me.

"So weak and ill I could scarcely stand, I clung to the door for support. All I grasped from what she said was the word *prayer*.

"I assumed she had come for help, and since my husband was away holding evangelistic meetings in another city, sick and dizzy though I was, I felt I should not turn her away.

"I invited her in and sank weakly to my knees beside the couch as she removed a damp scarf from her rain-bedraggled hair and laid aside her coat.

"As I started to ask about her need, she said, 'I did not come for prayer. The Father hath sent me to minister unto thee, dear child. He hath sent me to thee because of thy distress and great need. Thou didst call with all thy heart and thou didst ask in faith.'

"With that, she lifted me in her arms, laid me on the couch, covered me, and said, 'When thou didst cry unto Him in the night, thy Heavenly Father heard thy prayer. Sleep now, my child, for He cares for you.'

"Marveling, I said, 'Oh, thank you. But—how did you *get* here?'

" 'As the crow flies, came I unto thee,' was her strange reply. 'Because of the cry of thy heart in thy great need.'

"She asked if she might use my bathroom to wash. When she returned, she seemed almost a different person. There was no trace of her having been in the rain. Her thick auburn hair appeared freshly combed, with braids coiled softly about her head. There was an indescribable glow on her shining face, though it was a plain, sweet face.

"This was the last I remembered, for I, who had not been able to sleep for several nights, promptly slept. Only God knows how much I needed it.

"We had pastored churches in California, Michigan, and Iowa since our marriage, but had only recently come to Oregon, my home state. The pastor of the Assembly of God at Newberg had asked me to help with Sunday School and young people's work and house-to-house visitation, as I was able. My husband was holding meetings in surrounding churches while waiting for a pastorate.

"When he had been called for this revival, he had hesitated to leave me. My strength had not fully returned after the birth of the new baby—our eighth. However, I did not want to hinder his ministry. I assured him we could manage in some way, as the children had all been taught to work and were good to help me.

"On this particular Monday morning, after a sleepless night, I had fallen asleep about the time we should have been getting up and had overslept. The children and I had hurried through a quick breakfast, but took time for our morning devotions. Throughout our married life we have always tried to have Bible reading and prayer with all the children together right after breakfast.

"The two oldest children, Loren, a high school freshman, and Delta, our eighth grader, usually did the dishes; but this morning I had hurried them off to school. Delta saw my need and wanted to help but I thought she should not stay out of school another day.

"The children always took care of their own rooms and made their beds, but everything was topsy-turvy on this rainy morning because we had been so short on time. We agreed they could all pitch in and help after school.

"When the door closed after the last child, I was so exhausted I felt I could not go on through that day. The mountain of dirty dishes, the unmade beds, a cluttered house, and a large laundry overwhelmed me.

"I collapsed on the couch, hoping to rest enough to gain strength to bathe the two little ones, but had been interrupted by the woman at the door.

"Three hours later, when I awoke refreshed, I lay looking in dazed disbelief at my transformed house. All the children's toys and belongings had been picked up, and the floors were clean. My three-month-old baby, freshly bathed, was asleep in her crib. The dining table was extended to full length, spread with my best cloth, and was set with my best table service, with places for 13—plus the high chair for our 16-month-old girl.

"The appearance of the kitchen was even more

astounding. The heaps of dirty dishes had been washed and put away. The toddler, who usually was not still for a moment, was clean and sitting quietly in a chair by the table, playing with a spoon. *This she had never done!* There was a freshly baked cake, a large bowl of salad, and some other prepared food on the drain-board.

"Even *this* was not the most bewildering. The basket of baby laundry and a full hamper of family laundry, plus the bedding from all the beds that had been changed on Saturday had been washed, dried, ironed, and put away. My guest was just folding the ironing board.

"I stared in disbelief. My washing machine was certainly not capable of putting out that many loads in *three hours.* I had no dryer, and it was raining. How had she dried all those clothes?

"My usual three full baskets of ironing took me parts of two days and often the children helped to finish after school. Yet she had done it all. I found later that each child's clothing had been folded and put in the proper dresser drawers and that all the beds had been made.

"As I expressed my thankfulness and wonder at the transformation of the house, I asked, '*How* could you get so much done in such a short time?'

" 'It is not by my might, but God's enablements,' she said.

"I asked where she lived, where she had spent the night, and other questions, trying to find out who she was and where she had come from, but her answers were strange and impossible to comprehend.

"Finally, I asked, 'Why is all this food prepared and the dining table set? We ordinarily eat in the kitchen when my husband is away, and—we don't have *that many* in our family.'

"Her reply left me almost speechless. 'Oh, my child, you will be having guests soon.'

"I gasped. '13 at the table?'

" 'Yes,' she repeated, '13 at the table.'

"We talked in the kitchen for some time. I well remember my strange feeling of awe as she sweetly ministered to me in words of faith. I was absolutely confounded over it all. *I still am!* However, I know her words will never fade from my memory.

"As the children came from school, each took a look at my guest and came over near me. I could tell they were puzzled. Several of the younger ones whispered, 'Who is she, Mama? She looks funny—kinda different-like.'

"Earlier I had asked her name so I might introduce her to my family. She answered, 'Just say I am a friend, or a child of God who came because of your prayer.' So I told the children, 'This is a wonderful lady God sent to help me today. You see, Mommie prayed for help through the night, and God sent this wonderful friend.'

"When my husband returned quite unexpectedly soon after the children came home, there were five extra persons with him. There had been a death within the church, and the meeting had been closed for a few days. Since my husband had left our car for me to use, the pastor, his wife, their daughter, and another couple had driven over to bring him home. He would return later to continue the meetings.

"Our guest was just preparing to leave when Mr. Triplett came into the kitchen. I introduced her to him, as I had to the children. He sweetly said, 'That's just wonderful. It's just like Jesus.'

"At five o'clock when we were seated around the dinner table, with our six older children, the two of us, and the five guests, there were 13 at the table—plus the toddler in the high chair and the baby in her crib.

"Our guest vanished for a time, and we found all the cooking utensils had been washed.

"What could I have done, in my weakened condition, in my untidy house, without the help of this amazing guest? I would have been embarrassed to tears. My husband and family would have been ashamed, for we normally kept our housework done. The guests could not have felt welcome or at ease. What I might have been able to prepare for them to eat under those conditions, I do not know. Any woman who has been embarrassed by a similar predicament can appreciate my boundless gratitude to God for the help of this marvelous visitor.

"We could not comprehend what our eyes had seen. We had never heard of such a visitation. Though we *knew* it was *utterly impossible* for any human to do all that had been done in such a short time, in our fleshly curiosity and unbelief we questioned friends and neighbors, even the police in our small town, about the stranger. No one had heard of such a person and no one could give us any clue as to her identity. Our only explanation is that she was a ministering angel 'sent forth to minister for them who shall be heirs of salvation' (Hebrews 1:14).

"I have never been able to speak of this experience without being melted to tears at the unspeakable mercy and tender loving-kindness of my Heavenly Father to send help in my extremity. It has been so sacred I have not shared it often for fear others might scoff in unbelief. I affirm, as God is my

Judge, that *this happened, as related.* I had dragged through the days; prayed through the nights for strength to keep going; and *God,* who is alive forevermore, answered my prayer.

" 'O the depth of the riches both of the wisdom and knowledge of God! how unsearchable are his judgments, and his ways past finding out!' (Romans 11:33)."

There is a verse that should be reexamined carefully, for it is often passed over lightly without a great deal of thought: "Be not forgetful to entertain strangers: for thereby some have entertained angels unawares" (Hebrews 13:2).

CHAPTER THREE

Thru the Valley

"And it came to pass, that the beggar died, and was carried by the angels into Abraham's bosom."
Luke 16:22

Stranger, guide, messenger, avenger, guardian—all of these names describe an angel, but angels are also escorts in the life to come. They are often present at death. They have been seen many times by people present at the time of death or by those who were near death or passing into eternal life themselves. Some were comforted, some were healed, and some were escorted into heaven by the angels.

An angel came to 17-year-old Wayne Shultz one evening in answer to his prayer as he lay sick and paralyzed from his long fight with cancer. His mother, Loretta Shultz, is a longtime friend of mine. She told me his story:[1]

"Wayne had endured many restless days and nights, his sleep constantly disturbed by pain in his back and legs which he could not move. Nearly every night I would be awakened several times to tend to his needs, trying to make him more comfortable or perhaps read to him. His mind was very clear and alert; in fact, he often kept me abreast of the latest news items.

"One particular night, about six weeks before he went to be with the Lord, he asked me to pray with him a very special prayer that God would give him a good night's sleep. He said, 'I am so tired, and I just have to have a good night's rest.'

"So together we joined in prayer for a restful night. This time of prayer was so beautiful—the presence of the Lord was so real and sweet—we were just lost in communion with God. As we ended our prayer, I sensed a deep peace in my heart, and Wayne's face seemed to reflect this peace. I left the room for a moment to get a Kleenex to dry my tears. As I came back into the room, Wayne quietly said to me, 'Mom, I see an angel!'

"I stood stunned for a moment staring at Wayne, trying to comprehend what this could mean. I began to look around the room and said, 'Where is she Wayne?'

" 'Standing at the foot of my bed,' he replied.

"I was still again for a long time and noticed how peaceful he was as he looked at the angel. 'What is she doing Wayne?' I asked.

" 'She is just standing there looking down at me.'

" 'Wayne, I have never seen an angel. Can you describe her to me?'

" 'She's dressed in white, holding a lamp, and standing there looking down at me,' he said.

"There was such a peaceful feeling in the room that I just stood there watching Wayne. I was almost afraid to speak. Finally, I said, 'Is she saying anything to you?'

"He hesitated a moment and then answered, 'Her

lips are moving, but I can't hear her.' All the time Wayne was intently watching the angel.

"Then all of a sudden he seemed to hear her and he said, 'She just told me that God sent her to watch over me.'

"After a while I laid down on the couch and soon drifted into a restful sleep, only to awaken sharply at 5:30 with a sudden realization that Wayne had not called me all night long. This had not happened for so long that I was startled and began to wonder if he was O.K. I watched him to see if he was still breathing and asked, 'Wayne, are you O.K.?'

" 'Yes, Mom,' he replied. 'The angel was with me all night.' "

This experience was a source of great strength for both of them through the coming days.

All ages seem to have experienced the visits of angels. The little girl in Africa was only 10 years old. Wayne Shultz was 17 years old. Grandmother Smith also had visitors from heaven as she lay gravely ill in her old tenement building in Montana. Her story is told by C. L. Strom:[2]

"While in gospel ministry in Montana in 1932, I attended a fellowship meeting in Butte in April of that year. Following the afternoon service, the pastor asked me and one or two others to go with him to pray for an elderly lady who was ill. En route he spoke of what a lovely Christian lady she was. Stopping in a slum section of the city, we walked up 3 flights of stairs in an old rickety tenement building and down a long, musty-smelling hall. By this time I was wondering what we were coming to.

"On opening the door, it was as if we had stepped

into another world. I was immediately aware of the fact I was in divine presence—the Lord was there, as it were, to greet us—that is, I felt Him so near. It was as if an aroma of heavenly glory swept over my being.

"The pastor led the way into the next room, a small bedroom where 94-year-old Grandma Smith lay. In a rather weak voice she greeted and acknowledged each of us as the pastor made introductions. She went on to say, 'I have just been lying here talking to *Jesus*.'

"Then she related that just the night previous, she had visitors from heaven. She said her son (74 years old) who was staying with her had dropped off to sleep. She said she became quite cold about five that morning as the covers had slipped to the side on her bed. She couldn't awaken her son as he was soundly sleeping. She said, she just asked *Jesus* to send someone to help her right away as she was cold.

"Immediately two beings appearing as young men stood by her bed. They tucked the covers around her and then disappeared as quickly as they had come. She said she immediately recognized them as angels. She described how they were dressed and their general appearance. It was evidently a very real experience to her.

"She went to sleep right away. When she awakened, she felt well except for being a little weak. She had wanted to come to church, but her son had insisted she should wait a day or two until she was stronger.

"Two years later, I came back to that city. On learning that Grandma Smith was still alive and living in an old folks' home, I went there to visit her.

She was keenly alert and loved to talk about Jesus. I asked her about the angelic visit and her face glowed as she again related the incident of the angelic visit. Shortly after this she departed to be with the Lord she so greatly loved."

When Lazarus departed to be with the Lord, the angels carried him to heaven. This story was told by Jesus and recorded in Luke 16:19-31. A rich man wore rare, expensive clothes and sat down every day to an elaborate banquet of food while a beggar, Lazarus, laid at his gate full of sores and existed on the crumbs that were thrown from the rich man's table. The Bible says the beggar died and was *carried by the angels* into Abraham's bosom.

Dr. William W. Orr in his pamphlet *Are Angels for Real?* makes the following statement:

> Our Lord said that the beggar was carried by the angels into "Abraham's bosom," which was a well-known symbol of the highest place of blessing for an Israelite in the world to come. The Bible seems to indicate that at death, believers are transported from "this vale of tears" into the very presence of God.[3]

An interesting story by Leo Kirley from the *Herald of Holiness* tells of strangers—two men in white—who came to comfort at a time of great need.[4]

And Angels Came

"It was afternoon in Nampa, Idaho, where I was then a Nazarene pastor, when the phone call came from my niece in Rapid City, South Dakota.

" 'Mother isn't expected to live through the night,' she told me.

" 'Are your brothers there?' I asked.

" 'They both live in Washington now,' Mabel replied, 'and probably won't make it in time. I'm alone here at the hospital with Mother, but I can stay until the end.' Her voice broke.

" 'I'll be there as soon as I can drive out,' I promised, 'and we'll be praying for you.'

"While I prepared to leave early the next morning, my nephew Clarence phoned that he would meet me in Nampa and ride along. Memories of Mae, my eldest sister, flooded through my mind. Even though she was the oldest and I the youngest of the 10 children in our family and she had married before I was born, she had been special to me. . . .

"Late that night I began to feel a heavy burden on my spirit. I went over to the church and knelt at the altar to pray. In the quietness of the sanctuary the presence of the Lord came in an unusual way.

"As I prayed, I found myself, surprisingly, not interceding for Mae or concerning our traveling, but for my niece Mabel alone with her dying mother.

"I did not know if she knew the Lord, but I cried out, 'O Father, be present with Mabel!'

"Then I felt prompted to ask, 'And send angels to sit with her and comfort her.'

"The next morning early when my nephew Clarence arrived, I learned joyfully that he had recently become a Christian, and the long miles were shortened as we were able to fellowship in the Lord.

"We pushed hard, hoping that we might be able to get to Rapid City before Mae died. But late the following day when we arrived, we saw with one glance at Mabel's face that her mother had already 'graduated.'

"Clarence was first out of the car, and his sister threw her arms around him and began to weep.

" 'When did Mother go?' Clarence asked gently.

" 'Late last night,' she replied.

"Tenderly Clarence said, 'I'm so sorry you had to be alone when it happened.'

" 'Oh, but I was not alone!' Mabel stopped crying and lowered her voice, glancing around to be certain no one else could hear. 'I haven't told anyone else, but you and Leo will understand.'

"Her voice took on a note of wondering amazement. 'While Mother was dying, two persons dressed in white came into the room and sat there with me.' "

A Vision of Angels

Mrs. Edna M. Devin, a missionary for 22 years in Moluccas (Spice Island of Indonesia), tells how she saw angels around the crib of her own dying baby:

> Our baby died in Virginia Mason Hospital in Seattle in 1936. In my grief, as he breathed his last, I stood by the little bed. There I had a vision of six strong young men with arms folded, heads bowed, in the presence of Death, three on each side of his crib. I took these messengers to be angels, sent of the Lord to bear one little soul into the presence of God.[6]

The Ken Palmers, Conservative Baptist missionaries on the Ivory Coast of West Africa, tell another story of angel escorts:

> A few years back, an elderly Christian man known as Joseph was taken from the local hospital back to his village. He felt he would soon die and wanted to be home (in Tyengedougou). He lingered on, and every

time Ken was out in the village, he called upon him to see how he was and to help in any way he could. One day, just before church time, as he passed by, old Joseph said, "Good-by, my friend, the taking-away ones have come, and I'm going Home." When the church service was ended, they found him sitting there as always, but with the Lord.[6]

The apostle Paul said he would "rather . . . be absent from the body, and to be present with the Lord" (2 Corinthians 5:8).

A Christian lady saw a band of angels carrying her dear friend home to heaven in the following story which was published in the *Pentecostal Evangel*.[7]

An Angel Escort

"We had gone to the church early in order to be sure of a seat, for the speaker was quite famous, and this special meeting had been widely advertized. The church was packed out some half an hour before time for the service to open.

"One of the officers of the church suggested that we have a 'testimony meeting' while waiting, and I shall always be thankful for his suggestion.

"Among the first to speak was a lady just ahead of me, who looked like an efficient little business woman. She turned around facing us, and her face was so radiant, her voice was so earnest, that she immediately captured the attention of the restless audience.

"She said: 'I have had a wonderful experience this morning, and I wish to tell you about it. I dreamed last night that I was out in my garden looking up into the clear sky, sparkling with stars. Suddenly, in the distance I saw angels appear. They were white and glistening, and were flying two by two in perfect formation. They came nearer and nearer, not in a straight line, but in long graceful curves.' She tried to show us how gracefully they moved as they came nearer.

" 'To my surprise, they passed slowly over the home of my dearest friend, who was a saintly and devoted Christian. The angel at the head of the procession took my friend tenderly in his arms, as if she were a child, and started back toward the place from which the angelic band had appeared, the glittering procession following still in perfect formation.

" 'I was so overcome when I awoke, that I could hardly wait until morning, but as soon as it was light I hurried across town to the home of my friend's daughter, where she was living at that time. I rang the doorbell, and waited, trembling. The daughter came to the door and was evidently surprised to see me.

" 'How is your mother?' I asked, trying to speak casually.

" 'Oh, Mother is fine, or was last night when she went to bed; but of course, she isn't up this early.' "

" 'May we go up to her room?'

" 'Oh, certainly; Mother will be pleased to see you.'

" 'We went up to her room, and there she lay, cold in death, the peace of God on her lovely face. I put my arms around the daughter, and told her how I had seen her mother's glorious departure for her Heavenly Home with an escort sent from God.'

"I have forgotten the name of the great speaker who came and addressed the meeting, and I do not remember his message, but as long as I live I shall remember the thrilling story of the little woman who had seen her friend start for her Heavenly Home where the Lord Jesus, her glorious Redeemer, was waiting to receive her."

An angel appeared at the resurrection of Christ, which is one of the most gloriously spectacular and moving stories of the Bible. All of the sovereign supremacy of God, as well as a small portion of the glory and splendor of heaven, seemed to touch earth for a moment of time in that great Resurrection morning. The Father sent His representatives from heaven, clothed in resplendent white robes and surrounded with a light that shone with the brilliance of lightning.

On that first Easter morning Mary Magdalene and the other Mary came in the quietness of the fresh, cool dawn, just as the bright rays of the morning sun began to rise over the horizon. With sorrowing hearts full of reverent love and respect for their departed Master and Lord, they brought spices.

They did not know, as yet, that this was the heaven-appointed day for them to catch a glimpse of the majesty, power, and might of their Heavenly Father. They were to meet face-to-face one of the magnificent messengers of God and receive the joyous news of Christ's resurrection. On this day, they would be privileged to be the first to witness the glorious presence of the risen Lord.

Surely this first Easter dawn, the very air must have been electrified as they approached the tomb, for all of heaven's power had just visited there. Suddenly, they saw the brilliant celestial being who had rolled away the stone for them that they might see Christ was not there but had risen. This marvelous angel of the Lord brought a message for them straight from heaven above, as the Scriptures reveal in Matthew 28:2-8:

> And, behold, there was a great earthquake: for the angel of the Lord descended from heaven, and came and rolled back the stone from the door, and sat upon it. His countenance was like lightning, and his raiment white as snow: and for fear of him the keepers did shake, and became as dead men.
>
> And the angel answered and said unto the women, Fear not ye: for I know that ye seek Jesus, which was crucified. He is not here: for he is risen, as he said. Come, see the place where the Lord lay. And go quickly, and tell his disciples that he is risen from the dead; and, behold, he goeth before you into Galilee; there shall ye see him: lo, I have told you.

How their hearts must have quaked with fear, joy, and excitement as they turned and quickly departed, running to bring the disciples the glad news!

Death is just the glorious entering into the presence of God for the Christian. It was the psalmist David who said: "Yea, though I walk through the valley of the shadow of death, I will fear no evil: for thou art with me" (Psalm 23:4).

CHAPTER FOUR

In the Lions' Den

"My God hath sent his angel, and hath shut the lions' mouths."

Daniel 6:22

Fear no evil! No evil can befall us that God is not able to overcome. Daniel had no fear of the wicked men who plotted against him. He quietly went about his daily routine, knowing he was facing the lions' den.

The first words God's heavenly messengers bring at nearly every visit are, "Fear not!" The Lord himself so many times throughout the Bible has said: "Fear thou not: for I am with thee: be not dismayed; for I am thy God" (Isaiah 41:10).

God is with His people through all the hard places and especially in times of great danger. A. C. Gaebelein in his book *The Angels of God* says: "The great men of God in the past in every century record miraculous escapes from threatening dangers which they could not explain in any other way but by the ministry of the angels."[1]

That unseen protective hand of God intervenes in the daily lives of those living under His care, shielded many times by a literal wall of prayer—a mother praying for her children, a friend praying for a missionary.

To be a man of prayer is a noteworthy accomplishment. But, to be a man of prayer in the high courts of the land is an outstanding attainment. Daniel was such a man. Somehow he had escaped the corruption all around him. His blameless character had not been changed by the pressures of a high office. Daniel's appointment as the king's top administrative officer caused much jealousy among the governors under his jurisdiction, and they dreamed up a legal nightmare to destroy Daniel. But God intervened in his behalf.

Daniel had been taken from his own country as a young man and brought to the land of his captivity as a bondman. He was trained in the courts of the king as his wiseman and advisor. Daniel had refused to allow any bitterness or vengeance to abide in his heart because of his captivity, and the beautiful spirit within him had won him the love of the officers over him and the favor of the king.

Daniel had purposed in his heart to serve the Lord and remained steadfast in his faith in God even when surrounded by idol worship in a strange land. He was not dependent on circumstances for his faith. Daniel's great faith and love of God shielded him from despair and welded together a strong character that could not be bought at any price—even his own death. This was accomplished through prayer. Daniel knew the power of prayer. He had experienced it at crucial times in his life.

Once, when all of the wise men of the country were about to be killed because they could not interpret the king's dream, Daniel took the problem to God. He and his three friends prayed, and God answered their prayer with a vision showing Daniel the king's dream and the interpretation. For this the king made Daniel the ruler over the whole province of Babylon and chief of the governors over all the wise men of Babylon. (See Daniel 2:48.)

Daniel's faithful friends knew what it was to go through the fiery furnace for their beliefs and for refusing to worship the king's gods. Alexander Maclaren states:

> How small Nebuchadnezzar was by the side of his three victims! How empty his threats to men who cared nothing whether they burned or not, so long as they did not apostatize! What can the world do against a man who says, "It is all one to me whether I live or die; I will not worship at your shrines"? The fire of the furnace is but painted flames to such an one.[2]

Daniel's friends found that God was in their midst to protect them with a miraculous deliverance, for as King Nebuchadnezzar stood watching his men throw them into the fiery furnace the Bible says:

> Suddenly, as he was watching, Nebuchadnezzar jumped up in amazement and exclaimed to his advisors, "Didn't we throw three men into the furnace?"
>
> "Yes," they said, "we did indeed, Your Majesty."
>
> "Well, look!" Nebuchadnezzar shouted. "I see *four* men, unbound, walking around in the fire, and they aren't even hurt by the flames! And the fourth looks like a god!" (Daniel 3:24, 25, *The Living Bible).*

Daniel and his friends knew God had a reason for bringing them to this foreign land. Perhaps it was so these people might know the only true and living God. They were deeply aware of God's guidance. If God had put them here, He could take care of them.

They knew the Scriptures had prophesied the captivity of their people many years before and also the exact time of their release.

Daniel had an opportunity to reveal to King Belshazzar God's awesome power at a great feast the king made for a thousand of his lords. In the midst of their feasting and drinking the fingers of a man's hand came and wrote on the plaster of the wall of the king's palace. Perhaps it was the hand of an angel. Daniel was called to interpret the writing on the wall. He fearlessly told the king God was displeased with his wicked ways and that his reign was ended and his kingdom would be divided. That very night the king was slain, and Darius the Mede entered the city and began reigning in his place. It is an intriguing story from the Book of Daniel.

> Darius divided the kingdom into 120 provinces, each under a governor. The governors were accountable to three presidents (Daniel was one of them) so that the king could administer the kingdom efficiently. Daniel soon proved himself more capable than all the other presidents and governors, for he had great ability, and the king began to think of placing him over the entire empire as his administrative officer (Daniel 6:1-4, *The Living Bible*).

King Darius had placed Daniel as his top administrator of the land. This attainment was a source of contention among those calculating, ambitious governors and presidents who resented his appointment over them. In their unhappiness over Daniel receiving this high honor, they tried to find a way to get him out of office.

Often, a place of high position opens a person to attacks that would never occur otherwise. These men looked for something to criticize about Daniel to the king, but they could not find anything at all; for the Bible says Daniel had an excellent spirit in him and was faithful. Since they could find no fault in him, they dreamed up something.

These governors knew all the legal strategies and determined to use them to destroy Daniel. They plotted to trick King Darius with some ingenious and well-planned legal maneuvering, camouflaged with flattery and a pretense at honoring the king. They devised a new law (designed to get rid of Daniel for good) proposing to make King Darius a god for 30 days.

The governors gathered together before the king and greeted him: "King Darius, live forever! We presidents, governors, counselors and deputies have unanimously decided that you should make a law, irrevocable under any circumstance, that for the next thirty days anyone who asks a favor of God or man—except from you, Your Majesty—shall be thrown to the lions" (Daniel 6:6-8, *The Living Bible).*

The king, not being of a suspicious mind, was flattered into thinking they intended to honor him, and he signed the petition into law.

"But though Daniel knew about it, he went home and knelt down as usual in his upstairs bedroom, with its windows open toward Jerusalem, and prayed three times a day, just as he always had, giving thanks to his God" (Daniel 6:10, *The Living Bible).*

The men had been waiting and watching, hoping to find him praying to his God. So, they quickly went before the king and said, "Didn't you just make a law that no man may pray to any god except you for 30 days or he will be cast into the lions' den?"

The king answered, "Yes, that is true."

Then the governors and presidents said, "Well that Daniel, who was one of the captives from Judah, just isn't paying any attention to your law at all and still prays three times a day to his God."

The king soon realized his blunder and his misplaced trust in his lawmakers. Greatly displeased with himself for signing the law, he set his heart on saving Daniel from the lions' den and spent the rest of the day trying to think of some way to get Daniel out of this predicament. But soon all the men assembled before him again to remind him the law could not be changed or revoked. So, the king reluctantly called for Daniel and had him cast into the lions' den, telling him, "May your God, whom you worship continually, deliver you" (6:16, *The Living Bible).*

The king spent a sleepless night, fasting and refusing music or entertainment. He rose early in the morning and quickly went to the lions' den, and called with a loud voice, "O Daniel, servant of the Living God, was your God, whom you worship continually, able to deliver you from the lions?"

Then Daniel replied, "Oh king, live forever! My God sent His angel, and shut the lions' mouths, and they have not hurt me." The king rejoiced and Daniel was brought out of the lions' den, unharmed.

Obviously, Daniel's whole life had a special touch of the miraculous hand of God; no doubt, because of his devoted prayer life. Prayer activates the power of God. One angel who visited Daniel explained that he had started from heaven the first day Daniel began to pray (10:12, 13). Martin Luther said: "None can believe how powerful prayer is, and what it is able to effect, but those who have learned it by experience."[3]

Angels have a special ministry to mankind. C. Fred Dickason explains this so well:

> Scripture indicates that the ministry of angels to men is primarily external and physical, whereas the ministry of the Holy Spirit is internal and spiritual. Angels minister *for* us; the Holy Spirit ministers *in* us. (Jn. 14:16-17; Heb. 1:13-14) They guard our bodies and pathway; He guards our spirits and guides us in the right way. They may be agents to answer prayer, but He is the Prompter and Director of our prayers (Ro. 8:26-27; Jude 20).[4]

Isaiah 43:2 tells us:

> When thou passest through the waters, I will be with thee; and through the rivers, they shall not overflow thee: when thou walkest through the fire, thou shalt not be burned; neither shall the flame kindle upon thee.

Farmer Is Protected by Soldiers in White

Don Foster, a missionary to South Africa, tells the following story:[5]

> A farmer whose farm borders right on Mozambique and is in the present danger zone, had been advised by Security to move his family away because of the dangerous situation. He continued to work on this farm. Recently one night he received the warning signal that terrorists were spotted in the area. The farmer came under heavy conviction that he would be attacked, and became extremely fearful. This brought him to his knees where he confessed his errors to God and sought God's help. He prayed for 1½ hours before falling asleep.
>
> In the morning a truck with police and 1 terrorist explained how that they had intended attacking this farm, but couldn't, because the house was guarded by soldiers dressed in shining white. The terrorists were

afraid, and had run to the next farm where they were caught!

Not only is the Lord interested in protecting us in times of great danger, but also in the small dangers of life. He has sent His angels to protect us as His Word testifies: "They shall bear thee up in their hands, lest thou dash thy foot against a stone" (Psalm 91:12). How much He cares for us!

Child Is Caught by Angels

Curtis L. Dean, a missionary to Upper Volta, tells the following story of a young child who was caught up in the arms of angels.[6]

A young Mossi pastor had recently graduated from the Mossiland Bible School in Upper Volta, West Africa, when he and his family went to a remote village of Upper Volta and tried to open a new work. However, they suffered severe persecution. Rev. Dean explains:

"During those early months, only a few accepted the Lord. But the young man remained faithful in spite of the severe persecution in the village.

"One day his young son was playing when he accidently fell into the well. The father and the other villagers heard the young child scream and they ran and looked into the well. When they looked in, they saw the child sitting, as it were, on the water. The father, bracing himself against the sides of the well, slowly worked himself down until, at last, he could grab the arm of the child. With the help of the other villagers, he was able to get the child out of the well.

"Then came the surprise. From the waist up, the child was hardly even wet and the child said,

'Father, there were seven men in white garments holding me up out of the water until your hand grabbed my hand and then they disappeared.' That testimony and the evidence of this child hardly being wet stirred the entire village. The persecution ended and a large number immediately repented. Today the church is growing and prospering all because the Lord sent His angels to protect a young child from drowning."

Lois Covlasky and her husband, John T. Covlasky, have been missionaries in Alaska for over 20 years. She tells of hearing a voice that gave her lifesaving instructions:[7]

"I am a Home Missionary, born and raised in Chicago in a Lutheran Home on South Side. At the age of 14 my mother passed away from cancer. She was a devoted Christian and the Lord gave her great victory. Before she died she saw the same vision that Jacob had seen, the stairway to heaven and the angels.

"It was my custom in those days . . . to travel the streetcars to and from school and work, and I did not like to wait for everyone to get off before I ran across the street. One day, soon after I had gotten saved, I dashed across behind a streetcar on a north side street in Chicago and didn't see a big truck backing in reverse on the other side until I was right in the path of the truck, too far from the curb to jump, and only a few feet from the vehicle. All of a sudden without my knowledge or thought, my whole body lifted up and there I was on the sidewalk. I stood for the longest time trying to figure out how I could have gotten there. I know it was God's angel protecting me.

"Another experience was in St. Michael, Alaska. We were missionaries in that small Bering Sea Eskimo Village. I had noticed that my body felt so tired at times that it was even hard to find the strength to make my bed. I had no idea that my problem was diabetes.

"It was my birthday, and my father had sent a 5-pound box of beautiful hand-wrapped chocolate candy. I was alone in the house, a Quonset-type building which was our home, when I decided that I would eat all the candy I wanted. After all, we had not seen this kind of candy for years, and it was a special occasion. However, as I stood up, I felt there was someone standing close to me although I couldn't see anyone. Just as I placed my hand in the box, I heard a voice, plain and clear, say, 'Don't eat!' I was frightened and couldn't imagine what was wrong. Later, after we were financially able for me to have a check-up in Nome, it was discovered that I did have diabetes and would have suffered a severe coma if I had eaten that candy. I know it was an angel who warned me, 'Don't eat!' "

Young Man Saw Angels Flying Overhead

Edna Devin, a missionary for 22 years in Indonesia, knew a young man of simple faith who loved the Lord and eventually became a preacher. Some time after he had turned his life over to the Lord, he went to live with an aunt in the Puyallup Valley. He had to walk through a heavily wooded, very dark place for about 2 miles each night when returning from church. A real fear would take hold of him when he came to this spot in the road, so he asked very simply: "Lord, take away this fear and let me know You are with me." Immediately he heard a rustle overhead and, looking up, saw an angel flying over him, which flew as long as the dark spot was there! He was never afraid again.[8]

Protected by an Angel of the Lord

Cleo Tapp, superintendent of the Southern Missouri District Council of the Assemblies of God, gives this report of an event in his mother's life:[9]

"During the depression years of the early 1930s it was necessary for my father to be absent from home overnight upon various occasions. On one such night my mother was alone in the house with the smaller children in Illmo, Missouri, while my father, my brother, and myself were away. In the midst of the darkness of the night my mother was awakened by the sound of someone at the bedroom window. As she listened in fear she could think of only one avenue of help. She began to pray.

"Suddenly, there was a bright light at the foot of the bed and her immediate reaction was that the person or persons outside had shined a powerful light into the room. But from the bright light came an audible voice saying, 'The angel of the Lord encampeth round about them that fear him, and delivereth them.' She felt a great serenity of the spirit and no further sound came from the outside visitor. She fell asleep and awoke the next morning refreshed and safe. The angel of the Lord had kept and protected his own."

Milton Ahola, missionary to Japan, tells the story of a minister who was repairing his auto in Battleground, Washington, and was directly under the car when it fell down. A hand pushed him out from under the car. He bore the bruise of an imprint of a hand on his side. Surely an angel of the Lord was watching over him! Brother Ahola also tells of a minister's wife who was injured in a bicycle crash. While in the hospital in the month of March, she heard a choir singing a Christmas cantata. From that time on she had no more pain.[10]

Rev. Ahola personally heard the testimony of another minister who, when he was a young boy, was standing by a harvester being pushed by horses in the wheat fields at harvesttime. Suddenly the horses reared up and the boy was run over by the harvester, but he was not harmed. There were tracks next to him on both sides, but not on him.

In addition, Rev. Ahola recalls other incidents, such as angels being seen by men in a Georgia parking lot, angels standing over a sick person with swords, and angels surrounding a truck on the mission field.

As the Lord was with Peter in prison and on two occasions sent an angel to free him, so He is with His servants today. He is able to send His angels to protect His people from the perils of prison and war and from other dangers.

Only a minority, perhaps, has seen and experienced the ministry of angels in the midst of life's struggles. These individuals were not necessarily more holy or of a stronger faith than other Christians.

Only God knows the reasons why He dispatches those bearers of His blessing to some and not to others. But these magnificent strangers have been witnessed by people of all ages in many lands because the Lord willed it to be so.

CHAPTER FIVE

Guardian of Children

"Take heed that ye despise not one of these little ones; for I say unto you, That in heaven their angels do always behold the face of my Father which is in heaven."

Matthew 18:10

Henry Wadsworth Longfellow said: "A torn jacket is soon mended, but hard words bruise the heart of a child."[1]

Children are special! Jesus used a little child as an example. As a child believes and trusts implicitly in his father, so should we trust completely, unreservedly, and unquestioningly our Heavenly Father's love and desire to take care of His children.

In Matthew 18 special mention is made of children's guardian angels. Concerning this chapter A. S. Joppie says in his book *All About Angels:*

> This is rightly called the "Children's Chapter of the Bible." A child is mentioned seven times. . . . The disciples were arguing about who would be the greatest in the Kingdom. Jesus took a child and taught the disciples a very pointed object lesson. He informed the disciples that small children are recognized in heaven. If the Heavenly Father notes the fall of the sparrow, surely He beholds children.[2]

Jesus loved the little children and bade them to come to Him. Matthew 18:2-6 tells us:

> Jesus called a small child over to him and set the little fellow down among them, and said, "Unless you turn to God from your sins and become as little children, you will never get into the Kingdom of Heaven. Therefore anyone who humbles himself as this little child, is the greatest in the Kingdom of Heaven. And any of you who welcomes a little child like this because you are mine, is welcoming me and caring for me. But if any of you causes one of these little ones who trusts in me to lose his faith, it would be better for you to have a rock tied to your neck and be thrown into the sea" *(The Living Bible).*

To humble oneself as a child is simply to be aware of one's human defects and limitations.

Jesus continued: "Beware that you don't look down upon a single one of these little children. For I tell you that in heaven their angels have constant access to my Father" (v. 10, *The Living Bible).*[3]

Lukyn Williams believes this verse is speaking about "the angels especially appointed to watch and protect them—their guardian angels. This doctrine . . . that each soul has assigned to it by God a special angel, is grounded on this, and supported by many other passages of Scripture."[4]

Our Heavenly Father's special interest in the well-being of children is evidenced by many Scripture passages and by modern-day stories as well. For instance, as C. S. Osterhus relates, an angel visited some children in Ohio.[5]

An Angel Visit

John and Hattie Hittle lived about 3 miles from

Rossville, in the northern part of Drake County, Ohio, with their six children ranging in ages from 2 to 12. They were Christian people, and their home was for many years the home of itinerant preachers.

One night, in February 1887, there was a meeting in the neighborhood, and the parents and the eldest son went to the meeting, while the rest of the children stayed at home. They had never been left alone before and were a little uneasy about staying by themselves. However, their mother reminded them not to be afraid, for the Lord and His angels would take care of them.

After the parents were gone, they gathered together on the sofa for their family worship—except for the baby who was asleep in her cradle in the bedroom. After they had all said their prayers, they began reading *Foster's Child Stories of the Bible*.

Soon they came upon a picture of an angel, and Henry exclaimed: "Oh, I wish I could see an angel once!" All the children quickly agreed, saying, "I wish I could too!"

They had hardly spoken these words when they heard a sound on the porch like the rustling of silk garments, and there was a knock at the door. They rushed over to the window and looked out. To their great surprise, an angel came right through the glass! They were not at all afraid since the angel was pleasant to look at, and he began to talk to them.

He asked them about their parents, and they told him where they were. Then Lizzie, who was standing by the rocking chair, said to him: "Take the chair and sit down."

He said, "Oh, I can't stay long." But, he pulled the chair up by the stove and sat down.

The children noticed he was barefoot. Since the weather was extremely cold and the ground covered with snow, they naturally thought he must have cold feet. So, Henry said to him, "Put your feet on the railing of the stove and warm them."

The angel put his feet up by the stove and then called the children over to him. They were still wondering why he was barefooted in such cold weather, so they particularly noticed his feet, which were perfectly white and glistened like wax.

He took Ida on one knee and Nettie on the other and laid his hands on their heads as though he were blessing them. At the same time he talked to them, telling them to be good children and to continue to pray to the Lord.

"He had a most heavenly smile; his voice was tender and sweet; his entire demeanor was marked with gentleness and kindness; and his whole appearance that of grandeur and beauty." The children felt perfectly at home with the angel and were "enraptured by his presence."

After a while, he put them down, rose from the chair, and began walking around the room. His garment, which was loosely thrown around him, consisted of the finest white fabric and rustled like leaves or silk as he moved. He had large brilliantly white wings. Wherever he went, the children followed him, until they came to the bedroom where the baby was sleeping. He went to the cradle and took her in his arms and kissed her, then gently laid her down again, saying, "When Pearl gets older you must tell her to be a good girl and pray too." Then he said to them, "Well, I must go now," and he bade them good-bye.

As he came to the door, he paused a moment and they saw him glide out through the *unopened* door, in the same way he had come in.

Rev. Dustman became their pastor in the spring of 1896 and on January 7, 1897 was visiting the family in their home when he overheard their conversation about the angel's visit. A discussion had taken place in school that day of whether or not the Lord revealed himself to men now, as He did before, through angels. They remembered they had never before told Rev. Dustman the story so they described to him their angelic visitation. The pastor felt this should not be kept a secret, so the following day he wrote an account of the angel's visit just as the children had related it to him.

While visiting this family, he found there was still a vivid freshness in their memories 15 years after the angel's visit. They still loved to talk about their heavenly visitor.

Another incident of angels guarding children occurred during the great Indonesian Revival. The little children were so blessed they would form teams and go thru the jungle to other villages to tell of their wonderful experiences. Mel Tari tells about these visitations in his book *Like a Mighty Wind.* One day he asked the children if they were afraid to go thru the jungle by themselves.

They answered: " 'Why should we be afraid, brother Mel?' they asked. 'There is always an angel going ahead of us, and one on the right side of us, and one on the left side of us, and one in back. We just follow them through the trails, and they keep us safe.' "[6]

One special experience happened in the life of my friend, Mrs. Roberta Teeter, wife of evangelist-pastor Don Teeter. The Teeters were holding an evangelistic meeting in our church when Mrs. Teeter told the following story.[7]

It was New Year's Eve and she was just 16 years old. She and her friend were having a great time together singing and playing the piano. No thought of danger even entered their minds. They were babysitting two neighbor's children and her little sister at a neighbor's house just across the street from where Roberta lived.

They put the children to bed and sat down at the piano together and began singing some of their favorite songs. Suddenly, without any particular reason, Roberta got up and walked over to the little porthole window right by the door and looked out. To her surprise, she saw five or six older teenage boys hiding in the bushes below the front steps and watching them through the window.

The boys saw her at the same time she saw them and they instantly jumped up and ran to the front door. Frightened, Roberta quickly bolted the lock and turned off the lights. As she stood in the darkness, her next thought was to lock the back door. She tried to find her way, feeling with her hands in the dark, and running and stumbling toward the back door. The boys ran around to the back door also, but she arrived just a moment before they did and quickly locked it.

Roberta's friend didn't know what was going on, as everything had happened so fast. Roberta explained that a gang of young men was outside. About that time the young men began pounding on the windows and shouting.

The house had three huge, plate-glass windows, two on the front and one on the side of the house. The boys tried to break the glass. They banged on the windows until they began to crack.

The girls were frightened and didn't know what to do. Unable to find the phone in the darkness, they hid behind the couch and the rocking chair and started to pray.

Suddenly, Roberta's attention was drawn to a very soft noise, "like the soft rustling of taffeta," over her head and a bright golden glow. Looking up, she saw a large angel very distinctly. She could see his face, flowing hair, and two very large wings which were softly moving. Then, the angel was gone.

She and her friend got up and turned the lights on. Somehow they were not afraid anymore. "I'm not afraid anymore," Roberta told her friend.

"I'm not either," her friend replied.

Thinking the other might make fun, neither one wanted to talk about the angel. Nothing was mentioned about it for about 5 minutes. When they looked out the window they discovered the boys were gone. They wondered what the young men had seen that made them leave in such a hurry.

Finally, Roberta said, "Did you see what I saw?"

Her friend looked at her with a questioning look, "Well, what did you see?"

Roberta told her about the angel, and her friend said, "I saw the very same thing."

They excitedly shared with each other the details of the angel's appearance—the soft rustling noise, the golden glow, the flowing hair and softly moving wings. They knew God had given them His protecting angel to watch over them. To think He cared that much!

How great is God's love! He sees and knows the human fear in our hearts. He understands and cares. The story of a sorrowing mother is shared by Mr. and Mrs. Ken Palmer, missionaries to the Ivory Coast of West Africa for the Conservative Baptist Foreign Mission Society.[8]

A mother had given birth to a little girl and, as was customary then, spent several weeks recuperating in a nursing home. When she and the baby arrived home, she found one of her daughters (about 3 or 4 years old) had contracted scarlet fever and died.

The mother was very bitter, thinking that if she had been home to take care of the family, this loss would never have occurred. In her grief, she found it very difficult to care for the new baby.

One night, she awakened to see angels hovering over the newborn baby's bed. She knew this was a God-given message to her to love and take care of this baby, as she had the others. This assurance of God's leading and direction was a great comfort to her heart. From that time on, she was able to accept her daughter's death, as well as to lovingly accept the new baby, in whom she found a great deal of comfort and joy.

An angel kept Glenda Rogers from falling to her death. Mrs. Rogers writes:[9]

> God sent my guardian angel to protect me from falling to my death when I was 2½ years old. I was balancing on the foundation of our new home before the floor was built over the basement, and I slipped and fell toward the basement. But, I distinctly remember an angel flipping me over and placing my fingers in the cracks of the Mexican bricks.
>
> My folks came rushing over expecting to see me

crumpled on the basement floor, but instead found me clinging desperately to the wall like a bat. Dad pulled me up and spanked me for disobeying by balancing on the foundation. Evidently God knew He wanted me for some particular purpose. When I was 6 years old I asked Christ into my heart, and now my husband and I are returning to Zaire for our 2nd term as missionaries.

Jesus said: "Suffer the little children to come unto me, and forbid them not; for of such is the kingdom of God" (Mark 10:14). The Lord's great love for children is plainly evident throughout the Bible. God called Samson before he was born to serve Him. The angel who announced Samson's birth to Manoah and his wife told them he would be a Nazarite from the day of his birth, and he would begin to deliver Israel from the Philistines. (See Judges 13.)

The Spirit of the Lord rested on David when he was but a youth and enabled him to kill a lion, a bear, and the giant Goliath (1 Samuel 17). God also called Samuel to work for Him when he was just a child (1 Samuel 2:11, 18; 3:1). God's hand was on Moses when he was just a babe in the bulrushes (Exodus 2:1-10), and on Joseph the dreamer, whose dreams as a boy came true much later in his life (Genesis 37:5-10; cf. 42:9).

Several times in the Scriptures angels announced the birth of a baby. God had a special plan for each one of these lives. Four sons who were announced in this manner were Ishmael, Samson, John, and Jesus. The birth of John and Jesus were both announced by the angel Gabriel, "the mighty one of God."

An Angel Appears in the Temple

The time had arrived! Multitudes thronged outside the temple court. The prayers of the worshipers could be heard from the steps of the temple. Zechariah stood anxiously waiting to enter the temple. He had longingly awaited this day and carefully prepared for it. He was to perform one of the most coveted of priestly duties—the burning of the incense—giving the priest the right to enter the Holy Place, a privilege that would probably happen only once in a lifetime. This was truly an awesome occasion!

Zechariah walked up the steps to the richly ornamented marble porch of the temple—one of the most magnificent structures in the world. He marveled at the grandeur of the great gold-plated double doors and, stepping inside, he was awestruck by the beauty of the Holy Place. Rays of light sparkled from the pure gold covering the floor and ceiling, as well as the golden altar of incense.

But the room's beauty was not what made it so inspiring; it was the promise of God's presence, which would be in this place as long as His people served Him. The Holy Place was separated from the Holy of Holies by a thick veil, and it was there the glory of God had filled the temple with the cloud of His presence when Solomon had dedicated His temple. The Lord had promised Solomon: "I have hallowed this house, which thou hast built, to put my name there for ever; and mine eyes and mine heart shall be there perpetually" (1 Kings 9:3).

How sacred was this room, consecrated and dedicated to God!

Suddenly, Zechariah was startled and frightened by the presence of an angel of the Lord standing on the right side of the altar of incense.

"But the angel said unto him, Fear not, Zechariah: for thy prayer is heard; and thy wife Elisabeth shall bear thee a son, and thou shalt call his name John. And thou shalt have joy and gladness; and many shall rejoice at his birth. For he shall be great in the sight of the Lord, and shall drink neither wine nor strong drink; and he shall be filled with the Holy Ghost, even from his mother's womb.

"And many of the children of Israel shall he turn to the Lord their God. And he shall go before him in the spirit and power of Elijah, to turn the hearts of the fathers to the children, and the disobedient to the wisdom of the just; to make ready a people prepared for the Lord.

"And Zechariah said unto the angel, Whereby shall I know this? for I am an old man, and my wife well stricken in years.

"And the angel answering said unto him, I am Gabriel, that stand in the presence of God; and am sent to speak unto thee, and to show thee these glad tidings. And, behold, thou shalt be dumb, and not able to speak, until the day that these things shall be performed, because thou believest not my words, which shall be fulfilled in their season" (Luke 1:13-20).

The crowds outside were waiting anxiously for Zechariah and wondered why he was taking so long in the temple. When he finally came out he could not speak, so he motioned with his hands until they understood that he had seen a vision. When his time for ministering in the temple was finished, he returned home. Shortly after this, his wife Elisabeth found she was pregnant and rejoiced in the Lord for this long-awaited joy and answer to prayer. However, Zechariah was not able to speak again until after the birth of John (Luke 1:57-64).

A Heavenly Messenger

Six months later, the angel Gabriel was sent by God to Nazareth, a village in Galilee, to a virgin who was engaged to be married to a man named Joseph. He was a carpenter and a descendant of King David. The virgin's name was Mary. Luke tells the story of the angel's visit:

"And the angel came in unto her, and said, Hail, thou that art highly favoured, the Lord is with thee: blessed art thou among women.

"And when she saw him, she was troubled at his saying, and cast in her mind what manner of salutation this should be.

"And the angel said unto her, Fear not, Mary: for thou hast found favor with God. And, behold, thou shalt conceive in thy womb, and bring forth a son, and shalt call his name JESUS. He shall be great, and shall be called the Son of the Highest; and the Lord God shall give unto him the throne of his father David: and he shall reign over the house of Jacob for ever; and of his kingdom there shall be no end.

"Then said Mary unto the angel, How shall this be, seeing I know not a man?

"And the angel answered and said unto her, The Holy Ghost shall come upon thee, and the power of the Highest shall overshadow thee: therefore also that holy thing which shall be born of thee shall be called the Son of God. And, behold, thy cousin Elisabeth, she hath also conceived a son in her old age; and this is the sixth month with her, who was called barren. For with God nothing shall be impossible.

"And Mary said, Behold the handmaid of the Lord; be it unto me according to thy word. And the angel departed from her" (Luke 1:28-38).

How Mary must have wondered about this event; yet she believed the Lord. She didn't ask for a sign from the Lord as Zechariah had, but the Lord provided many signs for her along the way. The first one came from her cousin Elisabeth, whom she immediately went to visit. At the sound of Mary's greeting, Elisabeth's child leaped within her and she was filled with the Holy Spirit and prophesied to Mary about the Son she would bear. (See Luke 1:39-56.)

Angels had announced to Mary the birth of the Baby Jesus before He was born. They would also accompany His birth and His life here on earth.

CHAPTER SIX

Joseph's Dreams

"But while he thought on these things, behold, the angel of the Lord appeared unto him in a dream, saying, Joseph, thou son of David, fear not to take unto thee Mary thy wife: for that which is conceived in her is of the Holy Ghost. And she shall bring forth a son, and thou shalt call his name Jesus: for he shall save his people from their sins."

Matthew 1:20, 21

Angels appeared many times in dreams in the Scriptures. The Lord especially favored Joseph, Mary's fiance, with angelic visits in three different dreams.

A betrothal in those days was as binding as marriage and was customarily confirmed by vows and celebrated with a feast. Presents were given to the bride, and sometimes a ring was presented to the bride by the bridegroom. She was then regarded as virtually the wife of her future husband.

Mary and Joseph were pledged to each other, when an angel appeared to Joseph in a dream. The angel said: "Joseph, thou son of David, fear not to take unto thee Mary thy wife: for that which is conceived in her is of the Holy Ghost. And she shall bring forth a son, and thou shalt call his name Jesus:

for he shall save his people from their sins" (Matthew 1:20, 21).

When Joseph awoke from his dream, he did as the angel had commanded him and took Mary as his wife, but "knew her not till she had brought forth her firstborn son."

The Lord arranged, by a decree from Caesar Augustus, for Jesus to be born in Bethlehem. Everyone was required to travel to the place of his birth to be taxed. So, Joseph and Mary traveled to Bethlehem. There the Baby Jesus was born, as had been prophesied hundreds of years earlier.

Meanwhile, another miracle was taking place on the hillside overlooking Bethlehem. Shepherds were in the field, watching over their flocks at night; when suddenly, the angel of the Lord appeared to them, and the glory of the Lord shone all around them, and they were greatly frightened.

But the angel said: "Fear not: for, behold, I bring you good tidings of great joy, which shall be to all people. For unto you is born this day in the city of David a Saviour, which is Christ the Lord. And this shall be a sign unto you; Ye shall find the babe wrapped in swaddling clothes, lying in a manger" (Luke 2:10-12).

"And suddenly there was with the angel a multitude of the heavenly host praising God, and saying, Glory to God in the highest, and on earth peace, good will toward men" (vv. 13, 14).

When the angels were gone, the shepherds quickly departed and went to Bethlehem to find the Christ Child. How Joseph must have rejoiced at their visit as they told their thrilling story of the magnificent heavenly visitors. Joseph knew this Child was very special, for God had sent His angels to celebrate His birth.

The Lord also used a dream to instruct the three Wise Men who came to worship the Christ Child. They saw the great star and came seeking the king that was to be born. The Wise Men arrived at King Herod's palace, saying, "Where is he that is born King of the Jews? for we have seen his star in the east, and are come to worship him" (Matthew 2:2).

Fearing he might lose his throne, King Herod was troubled and called in all the chief priests and scribes and demanded they tell him where Christ was to be born. They informed him the prophets had written that Christ would be born in Bethlehem of Judea.

Then King Herod privately called the Wise Men and, hiding his true feelings, commanded them: "Go and search diligently for the young child; and when ye have found him, bring me word again, that I may come and worship him also" (v. 8).

Departing from King Herod, the Wise Men traveled toward Bethlehem. To their great joy, they saw the star, and it went before them until it came and stood over the birthplace of Jesus. Imagine the joy of Joseph as the Wise Men arrived and bowed down and worshiped the Christ Child, presenting Him with gifts of gold, frankincense, and myrrh. The men were then warned of God in a dream that they must not return to Herod, so they departed to their own country another way (v. 12).

After they had left, an angel of the Lord appeared to Joseph in a second dream, saying: "Arise, and take the young child and his mother, and flee into Egypt, and be thou there until I bring thee word: for Herod will seek the young child to destroy him" (v. 13).

Hurriedly, Joseph arose during the night and took Jesus and Mary and fled into Egypt, where they stayed until Herod's death. When Herod realized the Wise Men were not returning as he had commanded them, in an angry rage he sent his men to slay all the children 2 years old and younger in Bethlehem and the surrounding areas.

Years later, after King Herod died, the angel appeared again to Joseph in a third dream in Egypt and said: "Arise, and take the young child and his mother, and go into the land of Israel: for they are dead which sought the young child's life" (2:20). So Joseph arose and brought his family into the land of Israel, but when he heard that Herod's son reigned in Judea, he was afraid. And in another dream God warned him not to go there, so they went into Galilee instead and lived in the city of Nazareth.

Throughout the Bible, dreams were used to reveal God's plans for those who served Him—for the future of a life, a nation, and the end of time. The Lord sent dreams or visions to Joseph, Jacob's son. Joseph was called "the dreamer" by his brothers. Others who experienced dreams were Gideon, in the camp of his enemy; Solomon, Daniel, King Nebuchadnezzar, Cornelius, and Paul. One of the most outstanding dreams was that of Jacob. God showed Jacob the angels of heaven and renewed the covenant He had made with Abraham and Isaac.

He Saw Angels Coming Down From Heaven

The stars shown brightly in the sky as the hot

desert began to cool. In the quiet of the night Jacob lay down to rest, with a stone for a pillow. He was weary from his long journey and, perhaps, overwhelmed with loneliness and thoughts of home as he stared up at the stars and listened to the wind moaning sadly.

Jacob hadn't planned to leave home, but had to flee for his life from his brother Esau. He had cheated Esau out of his birthright and then deceived his father into blessing him instead of Esau. Now Esau was angry enough to kill him. Would Esau try to follow him and possibly find him in the middle of the night? What would this new land be like where Jacob was going? Would he like it there? Perhaps these thoughts raced through his mind as he drifted off to sleep.

How could he have stooped so low as to deceive his own brother and lie to his father to obtain his brother's blessing? Yet God, in His great mercy, still loved him and spoke to him in a dream. God was with Jacob and had been all along.

Eventually, Jacob fell asleep and dreamed a ladder was set up on the earth and the top of it reached to heaven. The angels of God descended upon it, and the Lord stood above it and said:

> I am the Lord God of Abraham thy father, and the God of Isaac: the land whereon thou liest, to thee will I give it, and to thy seed; and thy seed shall be as the dust of the earth; and thou shalt spread abroad to the west, and to the east, and to the north, and to the south: and in thee and in thy seed shall all the families of the earth be blessed.
>
> And, behold, I am with thee, and will keep thee in all places whither thou goest, and will bring thee again into this land; for I will not leave thee, until I have done that which I have spoken to thee of (Genesis 28:13-15).

Jacob awoke suddenly and was frightened: "Surely the Lord is in this place. . . . This is none other but the house of God, and this is the gate of heaven" (vv. 16, 17).

Jacob was far from perfect, and the Bible plainly tells us of his defects; yet God forgave him and called him to serve Him. Jacob later became the father of the Children of Israel. God even changed his name from Jacob to Israel. God calls men to serve Him just as they are with all their imperfections. He is able to change men's hearts. He changed Jacob from a deceiver to a "prince with God."

The Lord also reveals himself and His will in the dreams and visions of godly persons living in our present time:

> And it shall come to pass in the last days, saith God, I will pour out of my Spirit upon all flesh: . . . and your young men shall see visions, and your old men shall dream dreams. . . . And it shall come to pass, that whosoever shall call on the name of the Lord shall be saved (Acts 2:17, 21).

Pastor Sees a Heavenly Visitor

John Yeddah was sick and totally blind when he saw with his spiritual eyes the heavenly visitor in his home. His story is pieced together by several missionaries to Liberia. Lois Shelton relates the following:[1]

> I knew well the national pastor, John Yeddah. He was a precious man of God, fully yielded to the will of God. His eyesight failed and John became entirely blind. Young men from my station—the Bible training school—went to visit and "sorry" him as they say.

However, he would not listen to their expression, "No, no, children! The Lord knows what He is doing and He doesn't make mistakes."

. . . One of the joys of heaven will be fellowship with such rare souls as John Yeddah.

Missionary Anna Stafsholt, who served for over 37 years in Liberia and was decorated by the president of Liberia, tells the following story:[2]

John was in the ministry for many years. . . . He became blind, but was able to continue his ministry because he had almost memorized the New Testament and also knew many parts of the Old Testament. At times, he would have others read for him and then he would preach.

Two of the young students went over to "sorry" him, as they say over there, but he stopped them very quickly, saying, "Don't cry for me! God has sent His angels many times to talk to me. I'm going home, I am ready to go. Be sure you are ready to go."

Some time later, John became ill, and the angels came for him. One of the missionaries was in the room with him at the time. . . . Rachel, his wife, was doing everything she could to help when suddenly, he became quite excited and said, "Rachel, don't you see the angels? Rachel! Go back, or you will soil their wings. Oh, their wings are so bright."

He turned to the missionary and said, "You used to say you were white, but you are not white like the angels are."

John told them many things the angels had told him before. He recognized some of the angels as having visited him before and he talked to them. . . . The angels came and carried John Yeddah home.

John Begevch's Trip to Heaven

Missionary Anna Stafsholt also tells the story of a national minister, with whom she ministered for many years, and his trip to heaven.[3] John B. Begevch was a Sunday school superintendent in a town about 4 miles from where Anna Stafsholt lived. She heard he had had a near-death experience so she asked him to tell her about it.

"Oh, Miss Stafsholt," he replied, "it did not seem that I died, I am *sure* that I died."

He went on to tell her that at the time of his experience he could not read, but the pastor was helping him by reading the lesson and the Scripture passages to him and teaching him how to conduct the Sunday school. He was so hungry to learn how to do God's work in a better way.

One day he came home from working on the farm, and he was ill with a headache, chills, and a fever. He didn't feel like eating even though he had worked the whole day. He told his wife, "It is time to go to church, but I just can't go. . . . You go and tell the pastor and the people to pray for me."

He lay down on a mat in front of the little fire in the middle of their house. Suddenly, a shining white being entered the room. John said, "I never saw anything so white."

This heavenly visitor said, "John, I have come to take you to show you the place where you will come later."

Then John left his body—he didn't know how—but somehow he came out of his body, yet he seemed to still have a body. He was able to move around, but his body was still lying on the floor. He left the house with the angel and they walked through the village past the church. They seemed to be walking on top of the grass, then on top of the bushes, and then on top of the trees—until they arose up between the stars!

They walked until they reached the heavenly city. John had never seen anything as fine as that city. He described how large it was and said the foundation was inlaid with different stones, "fine, fine, fine stones." He had never seen any of these stones before.

Miss Stafsholt showed him some pins, including a pearl that had been set in a piece of gold. His eyes glistened as he recognized one after the other, and he told her they were the stones he had seen in heaven. Then he said, "There is something else. It looked like somebody had taken a handful of small fine stones and thrown them, and they didn't come down. They all stayed on the wall."

Revelation 21:19 says the walls "were garnished with all manner of precious stones." John had never read this, so he wasn't just describing something he had read.

The angel told him he had to go back to his wife and family. John looked down and saw them crying over his body. He didn't want to return, but he said he would do whatever God wanted him to do. The angel told him he should go back and prepare to be the pastor when Papa John came to heaven. So John returned to his wife and family.

Later on, when John Begevch died, his wife came to live with Miss Stafsholt at the missionary station.

John Begevch was one of God's chosen servants. The grace of God reaches out to all. James 4:6 says: "God resisteth the proud, but giveth grace unto the humble." And, in Romans 5:20: "But where sin abounded, grace did much more abound." Therefore, on the mission field the miraculous works of

God are often abundantly evident. These miracles are a sign to the unbeliever and a confirmation of God's love and presence to the missionary.

In times of old the Lord said: "If there be a prophet among you, I the Lord will make myself known unto him in a vision, and will speak unto him in a dream"(Numbers 12:6).

CHAPTER SEVEN

Gideon's Challenge

"And the angel of the Lord appeared unto him, and said unto him, The Lord is with thee, thou mighty man of valor."

Judges 6:12

The Lord makes His will known and speaks to His people in many different ways. God does not intend for His people to depend exclusively on angels for guidance. Although He sometimes sends His angels with a message of guidance, He also uses many other means to direct His children. Some of the methods recorded in the Bible are as follows:

1. *The Scriptures:* "Man shall not live by bread alone, but by every word that proceedeth out of the mouth of God" (Matthew 4:4). (See also Matthew 24:35; Colossians 1:5; 2 Timothy 2:15; and Hebrews 4:12.)

2. *Face to face:* The Lord spoke of His servant Moses saying, "With him I speak face to face!" (Numbers 12:8, *The Living Bible).*

3. *His voice:* A voice came from heaven saying, "This is my beloved Son, in whom I am well pleased" (2 Peter 1:17).

4. *The still small voice:* The Lord was not in the

whirlwind, the earthquake, or the fire, but in the still small voice (1 Kings 19:11, 12).

5. *Dreams and visions:* "God speaketh . . . in a dream, in a vision of the night," to seal their understanding (Job 33:14-16).

6. *Prophets and prophecy:* "For the prophecy came not in old time by the will of man: but holy men of God spake as they were moved by the Holy Ghost" (2 Peter 1:21).

7. *The Holy Ghost:* "For the Holy Ghost shall teach you in the same hour what ye ought to say" (Luke 12:12). (See also Acts 16:6; Romans 9:1; 1 Corinthians 2:10-13; and 2 Peter 1:21.)

8. *Preaching:* "It pleased God by the foolishness of preaching to save them that believe" (1 Corinthians 1:21).

9. *Signs, wonders, miracles, and gifts of the Holy Ghost.* "God always has shown us that these messages are true by signs and wonders and various miracles and by giving certain special abilities from the Holy Spirit to those who believe; yes, God has assigned such gifts to each of us" (Hebrews 2:4, *The Living Bible).*

10. *Angels:* "For if the word spoken by angels was steadfast . . . how shall we escape, if we neglect so great salvation . . . ?" (Hebrews 2:2, 3). "He shall send his angel before thee . . ." (Genesis 24:7).

11. *Circumstances:* "The steps of a good man are ordered by the Lord" (Psalm 37:23). "In all thy ways acknowledge him, and he shall direct thy paths" (Proverbs 3:6). "A man's heart deviseth his way: but the Lord directeth his steps" (Proverbs 16:9).

The Romance Made in Heaven

A perfect example of how circumstances can be a guide to God's will is the story of the search for a bride for Isaac. Abraham sent his trusted servant to his homeland to choose a wife for his son Isaac. Abraham told the servant the Lord would *send His angel before him* to assist him in his search for the right girl (Genesis 24:7).

Carefully preparing for his trip, the servant selected 10 camels and loaded them with gifts and provisions from the best of everything Abraham owned. Then he journeyed to his master's homeland and arrived at the village of Nahor (Abraham's relative) in the evening. He paused to rest by the village well just outside of town, and made his camels kneel down by the watering troughs. Soon the women of the village began to come and draw water.

Silently, in his heart, he prayed. He fervently wanted the Lord's guidance in the selection of a wife for his master's son. It was too important a decision for him to make by himself, so he asked the Lord to show him exactly which girl was the one He had chosen for Isaac.

He prayed: "This is my request: When I ask one of them for a drink and she says, 'Yes, certainly, and I will water your camels too!'—let her be the one you have appointed as Isaac's wife. That is how I will know" (Genesis 24:14, *The Living Bible*).

Before he had finished praying, Rebekah, the beautiful young daughter of Bethuel (the son of Nahor), arrived with her pitcher upon her shoulder and went down to the well to draw water. The servant ran over to her and asked for a drink from her pitcher. "Certainly, sir," she said, quickly lowering the jug for him to drink. "I'll draw water for your camels, too, until they have enough!"

The grateful servant watched her carry water to the trough for his camels. He marveled at her willingness to perform the laborious task of watering 10 thirsty camels; they drank an enormous amount of water after such a long journey!

When the camels had finished drinking, he presented Rebekah with a gold earring and two gold bracelets. Then he inquired about her family and asked if they might have room for him to spend the night. Rebekah graciously replied that there was room for the servant and his men to lodge and plenty of straw for the camels. The servant bowed his head and worshiped the Lord, thanking Him for guiding his journey. Rebekah excitedly ran to tell her family of their visitors.

Abraham's servant told Rebekah's family about his mission to find a wife for his master's son. When he finished his astonishing story, they turned to her and asked the emotion-packed question, "Are you willing to go with this man?"

Rebekah could see the hand of God guiding her life and already knew her answer. "Yes, I will go," she replied. So she returned with Abraham's servant to become Isaac's bride (Genesis 24:58-67).

Abraham's servant had asked God to take charge of the circumstances, and then he believed those circumstances to be the leading of the Lord. Abraham had reminded his servant, "He shall send his angel before thee," and God's angel had guided the circumstances all along the way.

Someone has said: "When a door slams behind you, look for the one God is opening."[1] However, sometimes the Lord does *not* want us to look at the circumstances, but only to Him.

Gideon had overwhelming odds against him. There was no human solution to his problem; he had to believe God. An innumerable host of Midianites had plundered Israel's crops and oppressed the people until they lived in poverty and fled to the mountains and caves.

One day an angel of the Lord came and sat under an oak tree. Gideon was threshing wheat, trying to hide from the Midianites, when he saw the angel. The angel said to him: "The Lord is with thee, thou mighty man of valor" (Judges 6:12). When Gideon complained to this heavenly visitor about all the troubles the Israelites were having with their enemies, the angel said: "Go in this thy might, and thou shalt save Israel from the hand of the Midianites: have not I sent thee?" (v. 14).

The Spirit of the Lord came upon Gideon and he blew a trumpet as a call to arms, and an army began to gather around him. But the Lord said to Gideon: "There are too many of you! I can't let all of you fight the Midianites, for then the people of Israel will boast to me that they saved themselves by their own strength! Send home any of your men who are timid and frightened" (Judges 7:2, 3, *The Living Bible).*

Fear is contagious and is the enemy of faith. For total victory the Lord wanted an army charged with faith. After this proclamation, 22,000 men left Gideon's army, leaving 10,000 still waiting to fight.

Then the Lord told Gideon there were still too many people. He was to bring his army down to the water and the Lord would show him which ones would go with him into battle. So Gideon brought the people down to the water, and the Lord made a division among them until there were only 300 men left in the army! By these 300 men the Lord would save them and deliver the Midianites into their hand.

During the night, the Lord again spoke to Gideon and told him to arise and attack the enemy, for they were already delivered into his hand. But, if he was afraid, he should take his servant and go down to the enemy camp; there his faith would be strengthened by what he would hear.

So Gideon and his servant crept carefully down the hillside. Through the darkness they could see that the camp of the Midianites stretched along the valley like a multitude of grasshoppers; so great were their numbers.

While pausing outside one of the tents, they overheard a man describing a strange dream to his friend. He said a loaf of barley bread had come tumbling into camp, hit a tent, and knocked it down. His friend replied that this must mean that Gideon, the Israelite, was going to come and conquer the Midianites, for the Lord had delivered them to him.

When Gideon heard this, he fell down and worshiped the Lord with a joyful heart. His fears and doubts melted and he returned to his camp with a new assurance of victory. Rousing his sleeping men, he told them: "Arise; for the Lord hath delivered into your hand the host of Midian" (Judges 7:15). Then Gideon divided the men into three companies. Each man received a trumpet and a torch concealed inside an empty pitcher. At the sound of Gideon's trumpet, they were to all blow their trumpets and shout, "The sword of the Lord, and of Gideon."

They surrounded the great camp of the enemy. Suddenly, the slumbering Midianites were startled by the dreadful blaring of trumpets. The confusing din of shattering pitchers brought them stumbling from their tents, only to be greeted with the wild shouts of the Israelites and the frightful sight of flaming torches blazing into the darkness from all sides of the camp. The Midianites imagined an enormous attacking army had surrounded them. Unorganized and leaderless in the darkness, they fought each other in wild disorder and fled in panic for their lives! The Lord had given the victory!

The Lord had challenged Gideon to follow Him completely. It is exciting to serve God and follow His plan for our lives, even when we do not know the outcome. If we follow Him, we will experience glorious victory, for He knows the end of the story.

Sometimes the Lord speaks to His people in visions. The following is a story of how God used a vision to challenge Louie W. Stokes, a missionary to Argentina.[2]

"I was a teenager, trying to serve the Lord in my native city, Atlanta, Georgia, but not always victorious and sometimes uncertain concerning God's will for my life. One day I was under the house where we lived, crawling around between the ground and the floor of the building. Without realizing what was happening, I was passing over the rotten boards of an old well, when suddenly they broke and down I went. Being alone, and no one aware of where I was, it seemed that I was a 'lost boy.'

"At that moment, I felt strong and comforting arms catch me; they lifted me up to the surface and placed me in a safe place. Was I happy! I have always believed that the Lord's angel was there, and preserved my life so that I could serve Him for many years in many places.

"The greatest experience occurred some years later when my wife and I resigned as teachers in the Bible Institute and began our travels, which have not yet terminated. We were engaged in a campaign, or revival meeting, in the Assembly of Phoenix City, Alabama, with Pastor Emory Andrews.

"One morning early, before daylight, I was praying in bed and seeking the Lord for the services. Without noise or words, in walked a majestic being through the wall. He moved quickly alongside the place where I was, and his penetrating, fiery eyes seemed to melt my whole body. I endeavored to speak, or move and flee, but I remained immobile. I was frozen stiff by his searching eyes. And then his words seemed to pass from his mind to mine, and this is what he made me to understand: 'These are the last days, and you have been chosen to go forth and announce the coming events according to the Prophetic Word, and to herald the return of the Lord.'

"Just as silently as he had entered, he turned and passed through the wall facing the street, and disappeared. For a while I could not shout or scream, but as my strength came back to me, I shook my wife, and with burning tears related as best I could what had happened some few minutes previously. The glory of the Lord filled the dormitory, and immediately I awakened the pastor and his wife. We ran out on the porch to see if anyone was there, but there was no sign of the large and lighted figure I had seen.

"As we have traveled in some 50 countries and

served as pastors and foreign missionaries of the Assemblies of God for several decades, this glorious vision has been a source of encouragement and consolation, for His angels do encamp round about those that fear Him and He defends them.

"In all these years, I have only related this experience some six or seven times, so it is almost unknown to others; a sacred and precious revelation of God's love and care for His children. Needless to say, my ministry was blessed in a greater way after having seen an angel of the Lord, and our favorite message is always, Maranatha, the Lord is coming!"

God's guidance and direction can be clearly seen in this story by Burton Pierce which appeared in the *Pentecostal Evangel.*[3]

More Than an Angel

"When angels appear on earth, do they look like men?

"Let me tell you of an experience that occurred this past summer, and then draw your own conclusions.

"On August 15, I was in Bessemer in Michigan's Upper Peninsula. My mother, grandniece, and I decided to drive to Duluth, Minnesota, over 100 miles away.

"Near Ashland, Wisconsin, we chose to take a state highway that goes along Lake Superior, rather than to take the more direct route to Duluth.

"We stopped in Bayfield for lunch, then continued on along the Red Cliff Indian Reservation. It was about 2:00 in the afternoon.

"When we passed a small roadside park at the

edge of the lake, I felt impressed to stop. But since we still had a distance to travel, I ignored that impression and drove on. Twelve miles down the road I felt the Spirit reminding me again and again that I must go back to that park. So we turned around and headed back.

"I admit I questioned the situation when I got out of the car and sat down on the grassy slope. There was no evidence of anyone else around. The three of us took advantage of the moments to rest and pray.

"Suddenly a man emerged from another part of the park, and I noticed he was crying.

"He walked directly to me and, after a few moments, said, 'You're Burt, aren't you?'

"We sat down at a picnic table facing each other, and he poured out his heart. Bill was half-Indian. He told me the tragic story of an auto accident in which he was involved in Oregon. His wife and only daughter died when the car plunged into a canyon.

"The day I met Bill he was so overcome with remorse and loneliness that he had planned to take his own life. The Holy Spirit had directed me to this man so I could minister to him.

"I encouraged Bill to look to the Saviour who could meet his needs. I quoted God's Word to him. I prayed with him. And Bill opened his heart's door and asked Jesus to come into his troubled life.

"I knew why I had felt so strongly that I must return to the remote roadside park. But one thing still puzzled me. So I asked Bill, 'How did you know my name?'

"I thought he might have heard me speak at a Men's Fellowship meeting, or perhaps we had met somewhere before.

"Bill looked at me strangely. 'Why, don't you remember?' he began. 'We were talking this morning down in the lower park.'

" 'But Bill,' I remonstrated, 'I was a long way from here this morning.'

" 'No, Burt, it must have been you. It looked just like you—except you had on a different color sportshirt. And you told me to come to the upper part of the park and wait for you.'

"I assured him it couldn't possibly have been me and told him where I had been at the time. Then he looked at me and asked, 'Well, where are you from?'

" 'I live in Springfield, Missouri.'

"He immediately replied, 'You told me this morning that you were far from Missouri!'

"By then all of us realized that the individual Bill had met that morning was not a human being but an angelic messenger sent to arrest his self-destructive actions until I could talk to him and point him to Christ.

"It was sobering to realize how long it had taken me to get to that park—and all that while Bill had been sitting, hour after hour, waiting for God's human messenger to come.

"If it were truly an angel in that lower park, then it was humbling to know that he looked like me. But more than that, it solemnized me to realize that the angel was sent only to arrest Bill's self-destructive impulses until a human being finally got around to being in the right place at a tardy hour to lead a needy soul to Christ. For to man—not to angels—God has committed the message of reconciliation."

Consider the words of the angel who rescued the apostles when they were thrown into prison for preaching the gospel. They were challenged to continue spreading the good news even though they knew it could mean another prison sentence:

> But the angel of the Lord by night opened the prison doors, and brought them forth, and said, Go, stand and speak in the temple to the people all the words of this life (Acts 5:19, 20).

CHAPTER EIGHT

The Battle Is the Lord's

"And Elisha prayed, and said, Lord, I pray thee, open his eyes, that he may see. And the Lord opened the eyes of the young man; and he saw: and, behold, the mountain was full of horses and chariots of fire round about Elisha."

2 Kings 6:17

Life is full of battles of every kind—spiritual battles, physical battles, man against man, nation against nation, good against evil.

Does our Heavenly Father ever intervene against evil forces to protect His children? Are there angel soldiers? According to the Bible and people living in this century also, the answer is a resounding "yes"!

Reports of angel soldiers protecting God's people come from all around the world. This story of angel soldiers protecting missionaries in Africa is from the booklet *The Ministry of Angels* by C. S. Osterhus.[1]

Angels Protect a Missionary in Africa

"One night a lonely missionary and his wife in the deep jungles of Africa retired, but could not sleep. They felt as though danger were approaching, but knew of nothing. They arose, however, and knelt down and asked God to protect them from any danger they might be in. Thereupon they retired and slept soundly until morning.

"In the morning a notorious bandit and murderer— the dread of the community—with his gang, came to the missionary and asked him if they could see that soldier guard he had around his house last night. The missionary said he had no soldiers there at all. The bandit, disbelieving him, demanded to search his house. He did so, but found none.

"The missionary asked him why he believed he had soldiers there. The bandit answered, saying: 'With my murder gang I was here last night. We came to murder and rob you, but the house was surrounded by shining soldiers, with sword in hand, of such size and strength and grandeur, that I and my gang quickly fled from your place. We had never seen such wonderful soldiers before in our lives.'

"The missionary then knew what had happened. In answer to his prayer for protection, God had sent a shining company of angels from the militia of heaven, who formed a glittering cordon around his home, and fully protected the missionary and his wife, their home, and their possessions."

In another incident, a Chinese woman from Shanghai was delivered from gunfire by strong unseen hands. Missionary H. A. Baker tells this story in his book *Heaven and Angels:*[2]

An Angel Moved Her Around

A missionary friend of mine was visiting a refugee camp. There she met a poor Chinese Christian woman whose heart was filled with overflowing praise for her miraculous deliverance by the angels.

She was living in her humble shack in the Chinese section of Shanghai when it was attacked by the Japanese. At the time of the attack this Christian woman was in bed. A strong, unseen hand picked her up, placed her in another part of the room, as bullets penetrated the corner from which she was so miraculously removed. A third and fourth time she thus was moved until she was able to escape. Philip was picked up and bodily carried away in Bible days, and God has never lost His power since then.

During World War I some soldiers experienced the protection of angel guards. James Check tells how some American soldiers went down into a shell hole for refuge. Around the shell hole bright angelic beings were seen. When the Germans tried to reach these men with their cavalry, "their horses became absolutely uncontrollable and ran away." The soldiers' lives were saved![3]

Many were the battles the Lord fought for the Children of Israel. An angel of the Lord came between the Children of Israel and the Egyptians at the Red Sea. It wasn't long before the Israelites watched the whole Egyptian army drown in the sea (Exodus 14).

As Moses later commissioned Joshua to fight their enemies, he challenged him: "Ye shall not fear them: for the Lord your God he shall fight for you" (Deuteronomy 3:22). And just before fighting the Battle of Jericho, Joshua met the "captain of the host of the Lord" (Joshua 5:13-15). He gave Joshua a strange battle plan to follow which, nevertheless, brought victory to Joshua and his men. There was no doubt about how they had won that victory. The Lord was fighting on their side.

There was also the time the Assyrians came to fight

the Israelites. First Kings 19:35 tells us the angel of the Lord went out and smote 185,000 Assyrian troops in one night!

Another time, King Ahab sent an army captain with 50 soldiers to arrest Elijah. But fire came down from heaven and destroyed them all. This happened twice, then the angel of the Lord told Elijah to not be afraid but go to the king (2 Kings 1:9-15).

A Host of Angels

One of the most intriguing incidents in the Bible is when Elisha was surrounded by a heavenly army of angels with chariots of fire.

The king of Syria held top-secret intelligence conferences with his chief officers to inform them of his battle plans. But Elisha, God's "man of the hour," repeatedly kept the king of Israel advised of his enemies' battle plans. Apparently, the Lord (or one of His angels) revealed this information to Elisha.

Finally, the frustrated Syrian king called together his chiefs and demanded to know who the traitor was in their midst that kept telling the king of Israel his secret plans. One of his men spoke up, "It's not us, sir. . . . Elisha, the prophet, tells the king of Israel even the words you speak in the privacy of your bedroom" (2 Kings 6:12, *The Living Bible).*

The angry king dispatched spies to find where Elisha was staying. Then he commanded a huge army, complete with horses and chariots, to surround the city in the middle of the night and bring back captive one man—Elisha.

When Elisha's servant rose early the next morning and saw the Syrian army surrounding the city, he was greatly frightened and asked Elisha what they should do.

Elisha confidently replied, "Fear not: for they that be with us are more than they that be with them" (v. 16).

Then Elisha prayed, "Lord, I pray thee, open his eyes, that he may see." And the Lord opened the eyes of the servant and suddenly he saw that "the mountain was full of horses and chariots of fire round about Elisha" (v. 17). The Lord had sent His heavenly army of angels to protect His two faithful servants!

The psalmist David wrote: "The chariots of God are twenty thousand, even thousands of angels" (Psalm 68:17). And, "The angel of the Lord encampeth round about them that fear him, and delivereth them" (Psalm 34:7).

As a young lad, David stood with a sling and challenged the giant Goliath:

> This day will the Lord deliver thee into mine hand . . . that all the earth may know that there is a God in Israel. And all this assembly shall know that the Lord saveth not with sword and spear: for *the battle is the Lord's,* and he will give you into our hands" (1 Samuel 17:46, 47).

David was only a lad, but God had revealed to him the secret to winning the battle.

CHAPTER NINE

The Missionary Journey

"And the angel of the Lord spake unto Philip, saying, Arise, and go toward the south, unto the way that goeth down from Jerusalem unto Gaza, which is desert."

Acts 8:26

David Livingstone said: "God had only one Son—and He was a missionary."[1]

The disciples of the Lord were also missionaries, going everywhere preaching the gospel to every creature. They needed direction from the Lord. He had given them an assignment, and He never gives an assignment without giving assistance. Angels were often present on their missionary journeys to help and to guide.

It is evident the Lord directed Mrs. John J. Friesen, missionary to South Africa. She has written the following story.[2]

An Angel Visits a Tiny Congolese Village

"I know He died and rose again because I've seen His power at work in heathen lives. The year was 1950. It was time to replace the five-year-old grass roof on our house in the Congo. But replacing the grass roof on a house is such a messy job. My husband suggested that I go with two other missionary ladies on an extended evangelistic tour in the villages while he took care of the roofing.

"For two weeks we ministered in village after village, telling the Congolese that Christ can forgive sin, transform lives, and take away the fear of death, evil spirits, and witchcraft. Many people had turned to Christ, and lives had been changed.

"Each morning before we started the day's safari, we prayed that God would guide us to people whose hearts would be open and hungry to hear the Word. One particular morning, as we drove along the hot, dusty road, we noticed a small trail leading off into the jungle. When we made inquiry about it, our guide acted almost uninterested. 'It's just a small village . . . there aren't many people in it . . . and it's a long walk,' he said. But in our hearts we felt impelled to follow that path.

"Leaving the car, we started down the trail on foot. The guide had been right . . . it was a long and very hot walk, and we found only a small clearing in the bush, with just a few huts. But the people who were there gathered quickly and gladly when we told them we had come with 'Good News.'

"On a grass mat in the shade of a mango tree sat a little old grandmother, naked except for her 'negbe' (grass skirt). When the invitation was given for those who wanted to accept Jesus as Saviour and Friend, she was the first to respond. As the pastor who was traveling with us spoke with her and prayed with her, she understood and responded wholeheartedly. For one of her age to accept Jesus as Saviour the very first time she heard the gospel was most unusual.

"*But then we heard her story.*

"Talking loudly and with great excitement, she

told us, 'Last night I was asleep on the grass mat by the fire in my hut. As I lay there, a man dressed in shining white garments stood by my side, and looking down at me, said, "Mama, tomorrow you will hear wonderful news!" His words are true! The sun is not yet high overhead, and you have come to tell me the Good News about Jesus!'

"Her heart had been prepared, she had heard the message, and there in that tiny Congolese village had become a child of God. She knew by experience that Jesus came and died and rose again, for she felt His peace in her heart!"

In *The Great Doctrines of the Bible*, William Evans says about angels: "They guide the worker to the sinner (Acts 8:26) and the sinner to the worker (Acts 10:3.)"[3]

This kind of guidance took place in the story of Philip and the Ethiopian (Acts 8:26-40). An angel of the Lord told Philip exactly where to go to find a searching heart. He was to travel south to a particular road that leads from Jerusalem to the Gaza Desert. The angel told Philip *where* he was to go, but not *what* he should do when he arrived. Sometimes we must follow our Heavenly Father's guidance one step at a time.

After Philip had followed his instructions and arrived on the scene, he was given further instructions (v. 29). He was to speak to an Ethiopian man, the treasurer to the queen of Ethiopia, who had come to Jerusalem to worship and was reading the Scriptures. God had planned this meeting and had sent His angel to direct their paths.

Another fascinating story of divine guidance is

found in Acts 10. An angel appeared to Cornelius, a Roman army officer, in a vision. The angel told him to send men to Joppa to find Peter and ask him to come and give him further enlightenment from God's Word. The angel knew Cornelius' name and all about his prayers and alms:

> Cornelius. . . . Thy prayers and thine alms are come up for a memorial before God. And now send men to Joppa, and call for one Simon, whose surname is Peter: he lodgeth with one Simon a tanner, whose house is by the sea side: he shall tell thee what thou oughtest to do (10:3-6).

The angel had told him to send men to a specific town (Joppa), for a certain man (Peter), who lodged in a particular house by the sea. And this, of course was exactly where Peter was found. God had also prepared Peter's heart. How could any guidance be more exact than that?

Hetyo Has a Heavenly Visitor

An angelic being also directed Hetyo, an elderly woman of West Africa. Her story and her brother's story are told by Mr. and Mrs. Ken Palmer:[4]

"In 1939 or 1940, when the work among the Dyimini—a people of the great Senufo nation—began, there was an angelic visitation to an old woman of the village of Tyengedougou (Cheh-ngey-dugu), some 30 kilometers from where we live.

"Hetyo (Hey-cho) an elderly woman, past her prime, was in an abandoned old hut with a leaky straw roof. She suffered from an ulcerous condition of her leg that prevented her hobbling about but very little. One night she said a visitor in shining white came to her—although she wasn't sure if it was just a dream—and said, 'Old woman, if you would be made well, go south.'

"She pondered the meaning of this vision, or visitation, but continued to pay out of her meager supplies to the witch doctors for the healing of her limb. After several months, she was relating this story to a son-in-law who, astonished at her remaining and doling out her money to the fetishists, cried out, 'That was God speaking to you. What are you waiting for?'

"Hetyo put her worldly belongings into a basket on her head, and with cane in hand to help her, hobbled the 80 kilometers straight south to the large city of Bouake. It took her 3 days to make the trip. It was a Sunday when she arrived at the marketplace, heard the gospel being preached, and was gloriously saved. She then went to the C&MA mission station where they took care of her sores.

"A few months later, in good health and strength, she returned to her village, calling to all as she entered. Most thought she had gone out to the bush to die. She told them her amazing story, and that night many were brought to a personal knowledge of the Saviour.

"The work we are in is a direct result of all that, although we didn't arrive on the field until some 9 years later, and then it was 5 more years before we got down to Dabakala to work among these people, many of whom are related to her. She paid with her life for her testimony, but that didn't alter God's plan and the progress of the gospel in the area. . . .

"Hetyo also had a brother who lived to be an old, old man. About 3 years ago, he became ill and longed to go home to heaven. When he was visiting with others, suddenly he would cock his head, listening, and say, 'Don't you hear them? The angels are coming.'

"He was certain the heavenly host was approaching and he was to go with them. As he listened to the angelic singing, he wondered that others could not share its beauty with him. God's own heavenly escorts came to see that he got home all right."

Mark Buntain, a legend in India because of his work with the people there, is an Assemblies of God missionary whose church has a membership of over 7,000. This church conducts seven services each Sunday, has a radio studio, hospital, village ministry, and correspondence institute. Rev. Buntain tells the following story:[5]

> We recently had a wonderful experience in our Dum Dum Church, about 15 miles from Calcutta, when a Brahmin Hindu *who did not know the gospel* was at the point of death. His bed was in such a position that he could look through the window towards our church. Just when it seemed he was passing away he looked towards the church and Jesus Himself appeared to him. With the Lord were two of His angels. The Lord instructed them to go and heal that man. . . .
>
> He [the Hindu man] began shouting, "Jesus Christ has healed me, Jesus Christ has healed me. He sent two young men and they have taken my sickness away." He kept on exclaiming, "Jesus Christ is the living God, Jesus Christ is the living God."

Another missionary, Walter E. Erickson, met a stranger who supplied a very real need. He relates the following story:[6]

"We had been weeks on the trail, evangelizing in the Peruvian Andes. We had crossed the great Continental Divide to where all the rivers drain into the headwaters of the Amazon. We were tired from many weeks in the saddle, and our mules were tired.

"We rode into a small town looking for lodging. These simple mountain people are more than hospitable, but we found no feed for our mules. This is as important as gasoline for an auto. However, we were told that higher up the mountainside we would find natural forage for our animals, a coarse wiregrass which grows profusely at high altitudes, and that there was a cave where we could pass the night.

"It was late in the afternoon when we came to the place they had indicated, but it was not a cave. Rather, it was a huge boulder lodged on the mountainside, under the edge of which it was possible to find some shelter from the elements. However, a pack train had already arrived with three or four mule drivers and perhaps 20 or 30 mules, carrying produce from the distant coast to the interior. They occupied all the available space, so we decided to continue to climb, and see if we could find something farther up the mountainside.

"We were getting up into the higher altitudes, perhaps 15,000 feet above sea level, recrossing the great Continental Divide, to return to our home base. It began to snow, and I dismounted to see if we could find some kind of shelter in the lee of a boulder, when out of the snow storm came an Indian, heading down the mountain. We have frequently seen the Indians as they travel. Usually a couple of men, a woman, and perhaps a donkey with a child tied in the saddle. It was a common sight, but some way, this one was different. He was traveling alone and paused only long enough to tell us that there was a cave a couple of blocks further up the mountain, and he disappeared into the snow storm.

"I remounted and we continued to climb, and there, as he had said, just off the trail to the left, we found the cave. It was about as big as the space under a good sized table, perhaps 6 feet across or so, and maybe 30 inches inside. It was far from comfortable, but it was dry. We pulled the saddles from our mules and turned them loose to forage as best they could. The snow eventually ceased, but it continued to rain all night. We would have spent a most uncomfortable night had we tried to find shelter from the inclement weather under the edge of a boulder. It was the timely arrival of our visitor which saved the situation.

"But, I ask myself, was he an Indian, or was he an angel sent from God? It might easily have been the latter. You try sleeping in the open, high in the Peruvian Andes at possibly close to 15,000 feet in a storm of rain and snow, and you will more fully understand what I mean.

"A number of years have passed since that afternoon, but I frequently wonder about our visitor, because I do know that the Lord still has His angels to watch over His children."

These celestial beings at times even lend a helping hand to the missionary. A heavenly visitor helped to place a heavy cement beam in a church in the following incident related by Assemblies of God missionary B. T. Bard:[7]

"Traveling in the Inland from Shansi Province to Peking, China, I used to stop in Shih Chia Chuang. Here Peter Rasmussen, a Danish missionary, was faithfully laboring for the Lord. They built a nice church, where about 300 Christians gathered for worship.

"Showing me this edifice from the outside, Rev. Rasmussen called my attention to a long heavy *concrete* beam high over the entrance of the church. He told me it took much thought and labor to get it way up there. As they had no modern equipment, they had to put up a scaffold.

"With very heavy ropes pulled by many strong men, they succeeded finally in hoisting the beam to place it on top of the already erected wall. Rev. Rasmussen watched the beam being pulled up. They hoisted the beam as far as it would go. Then to his great grief and disappointment he could see that it still lacked a little more height to put it in its place. As he was wondering what could be done, he looked up and saw that the heavy beam had landed in the right place. He couldn't figure out how this could have happened.

"Later on, during the meeting in the church, one of the Christian women rose up to testify. She related that she was present when the beam was being hoisted and that she had seen an angel lift and place the beam in its proper place.

"This isn't the first time that angels have used their hands to move heavy objects. Didn't Matthew inform us that an angel descended from heaven and rolled back the stone from the door of the sepulchre of our risen Lord and Saviour (Matthew 28:2)?"

When Jesus appeared to his disciples a short time

after His resurrection, He told them: "Go ye into all the world, and preach the gospel to every creature" (Mark 16:15).

What is the gospel message? The simple story of God's love told in John 3:16: "For God so loved the world, that he gave his only begotten Son, that whosoever believeth in him should not perish, but have everlasting life."

Romans 10:13 tells us: "For whosoever shall call upon the name of the Lord shall be saved." Then the question is asked: "How then shall they call on him whom they have not believed? and how shall they believe in him of whom they have not heard? and how shall they hear without a preacher?" (v. 14).

The Lord has sent prophets, preachers, and missionaries to tell the glad news, and angels as helpers, avengers, guides, messengers, guardians, and escorts.

CHAPTER TEN

Trumpet Sounds

"And he shall send his angels with a great sound of a trumpet, and they shall gather together his elect from the four winds, from one end of heaven to the other."

Matthew 24:31

Two strangers with good news disappeared from a speeding car in California. Hymman O. Wood, missionary to Nigeria, tells the story of an experience of his uncle, the late Lawrence Wood of Fresno, California.

Rev. Wood was driving alone on Highway 99 in Central California when he saw two hitchhikers who appeared to be very average men, so he gave them a lift. As they traveled, the conversation got around to the coming of the Lord. Rev. Wood said:

> They confirmed my feeling that He was coming soon by assuring me that it was true. We were traveling at about 50 miles per hour, still discussing His Coming, when suddenly they were gone. I did not see them go, nor were the doors of the car open or shut. They literally disappeared.[1]

The angels will herald Christ's return with the sound of the trumpet. Matthew 24:31 tells us: "And he shall send his angels with a great sound of a trumpet, and they shall gather together his elect from the four winds, from one end of heaven to the other."

The return of the Christ, the Messiah, the Anointed One, the very Son of God! He is the Redeemer of all mankind of whom the prophets of the Lord wrote about from the beginning of time. They recorded hundreds of prophecies which were fulfilled many years later during the life of Christ.[2]

The apostles also testified of the living Christ. Peter said: "For we have not followed cunningly devised fables, when we made known unto you the power and coming of our Lord Jesus Christ, but were eyewitnesses of his majesty" (2 Peter 1:16). And John testified: "I myself have seen him with my own eyes and listened to him speak. I have touched him with my own hands. He is God's message of Life" (1 John 1:1, *The Living Bible).*

The angels confirmed God's glorious message to this world:

To Joseph the angel announced Jesus as the Saviour: "Thou shalt call his name Jesus: for he shall save his people from their sins" (Matthew 1:21).

To Mary the angel presented Jesus as the coming King: "Thou . . . shalt call his name Jesus. He shall be great, and shall be called the Son of the Highest; . . . and of his kingdom there shall be no end" (Luke 1:31-33).

To the shepherds the angel said: "Fear not: for, behold, I bring you good tidings of great joy, which shall be to all people. For unto you is born this day in the city of David a Saviour, which is Christ the Lord" (Luke 2:10, 11).

To Mary Magdalene and the other Mary at the

sepulchre the angel said: "He is not here: for he is risen" (Matthew 28:6).

To the apostles at the Ascension the angels said: "Ye men of Galilee, why stand ye gazing up into heaven? this same Jesus, which is taken up from you into heaven, shall so come in like manner as ye have seen him go into heaven" (Acts 1:11).

We also have the promise: "The Lord himself shall descend from heaven with a shout, with the voice of the archangel, and with the trump of God: and the dead in Christ shall rise first: then we which are alive and remain shall be caught up together with them in the clouds, to meet the Lord in the air: and so shall we ever be with the Lord" (1 Thessalonians 4:16, 17).

These magnificent strangers have been sent to convey the message that one day this glorious, majestic Christ will come again in all His splendor and reign over the whole earth. As Matthew says: "When the Son of man shall come in his glory, and all the holy angels with him, then shall he sit upon the throne of his glory" (Matthew 25:31).

Finally, in the words of the apostle Paul: "That at the name of Jesus every knee should bow, of things in heaven, and things in earth, and things under the earth; and that every tongue should confess that Jesus Christ is Lord, to the glory of God the Father" (Philippians 2:10, 11).

[illegible] angels [illegible]
[illegible]
[illegible] the [illegible] of the [illegible]
[illegible] [illegible] stand [illegible]
[illegible]
[illegible] into [illegible]

[illegible] sound from heaven [illegible] the voice of the [illegible] and the [illegible] shall [illegible] together [illegible] them to [illegible]

[illegible] come [illegible] whole earth [illegible]
[illegible]
the [illegible] in earth and [illegible] every tongue should confess that Jesus [illegible] Lord, to the glory of God the Father. (Philippians 2:10, 11)

Notes

Foreword

[1]From *Audrey Mieir–The Laughter and the Tears* by Audrey Mieir. Copyright 1976 by Manna Music, Inc., 2111 Kenmere Avenue, Burbank, CA 91504. International copyright secured. All rights reserved. Used by permission.

[2]*Beyond and Back* by Ralph Wilkerson. Bantam Books, Inc., New York. Copyright 1977 by Ralph Wilkerson.

[3]Billy Graham, *Angels: God's Secret Agents*. New York: Doubleday & Co., 1975.

[4]Betty Malz, *My Glimpse of Eternity*. Old Tappan, NJ: Chosen Books, 1977.

[5]From *Norma* by Norma Zimmer. Copyright 1976 by Tyndale House Publishers, Inc., Wheaton, Illinois. Used by permission.

Chapter 1

[1]Gladys Wolverton, missionary to South Africa, letter to author, November 27, 1973.

[2]*Ibid.*

[3]Ruth Rill, missionary to Africa, telephone interview, Sacramento, California, 1974.

[4]Wanda Moore, missionary to the Congo, letter to author, January 23, 1974.

[5]From V. *Raymond Edman: In the Presence of the King* by Earle E. Cairns. Copyright 1972. Moody Press, Moody Bible Institute of Chicago. Used by permission.

[6]From *Marching Orders for the End Battle* by Corrie ten Boom. Christian Literature Crusade, Inc. Used by permission.

[7]Reprinted from the *Pentecostal Evangel* by permission. Copyright 1973 by The General Council of the Assemblies of God.

[8]Gail Winters, missionary to the Republic of Zaire, letter to author, July 31, 1974.

Chapter 2

[1]From *Angels, Angels, Angels* by Landrum P. Leavell. Nashville, TN: Broadman Press, copyright 1973, p. 19.

[2]From *All About Angels* by C. Leslie Miller. Glendale, CA: Gospel Light Publications, Regal Books Division, copyright 1973, p. 12.

[3]From *Systematic Theology* by Lewis Sperry Chafer, D.D., Litt. D. Dallas: Dallas Seminary Press, copyright 1947, p. 12.

[4]From *Clarke's Commentary* by Adam Clarke, LL.D., F.S.A. New York: Abingdon-Cokesbury Press, Vol. I, p. 118.

[5]Wanda Cummings, manuscript and tape recording sent to author, January 26, 1975.

[6]Carol Corpany, *Middle East Outreach Reporter*, Vol. 1, No. 1, 1973. Used by permission.

[7]Gladys Triplett as told to Emma Claypool Moore, "13 at the Table," *Live*, July 21, 1968. Springfield, MO: Gospel Publishing House. Used by permission.

Chapter 3

[1]Loretta Shultz, personal interview, Sacramento, California, May 19, 1976.

[2]C. L. Strom, letter to author, January 27, 1974.

[3]From *Are Angels for Real?* by William W. Orr. Wheaton, IL: Scripture Press Publications, Inc., copyright 1970, p. 28.

[4]"And Angels Came," by Rev. Leo Kirley as told to Virginia Kirley Leih, *Herald of Holiness*, Vol. 63, No. 21, October 9, 1974, pp. 12, 13. Kansas City, MO: Nazarene Publishing House. Used by permission.

[5]Edna Devin, missionary to Moluccas, letter to author, October 9, 1973.

[6]Mr. and Mrs. Ken Palmer, missionaries to West Africa, letter to author, September 26, 1974.

[7]A true story by Elizabeth Bowman. Reprinted from the *Pentecostal Evangel* by permission. Copyright 1973 by The General Council of the Assemblies of God.

Chapter 4

[1]From *The Angels of God* by A. C. Gaebelein. Grand Rapids: Baker Book House, reprinted 1969, p. 98.

[2]From *Expositions of Holy Scripture* by Alexander Maclaren, D.D., Litt.D. Grand Rapids: Wm. B. Eerdmans Publishing Co., 1944, Vol. VI, p. 60.

[3]From *Sourcebook for Speakers* by Eleanor Doan. Grand Rapids: Zondervan Publishing House, 1968.

[4]From *Angels Elect and Evil* by C. Fred Dickason. Chicago: Moody Press, 1975.

[5]From *Christian Mission to the Communist World* newsletter. Glendale, CA: May 21, 1976.

[6]Curtis L. Dean, missionary to Africa, letter to author, November 23, 1977.

[7]Lois Covlasky, missionary to Alaska, letter to author, January 31, 1974.

[8]Edna M. Devin, missionary to Moluccas (Spice Island) of Indonesia, letter to author, October 9, 1973.

[9]N. Cleo Tapp, superintendent of the Southern Missouri District Council of the Assemblies of God, letter to author, November 6, 1973.

[10]Milton Ahola, missionary to Japan, personal interview, Sacramento, California, May 5, 1974.

Chapter 5

[1]From *1000 Stories and Quotations of Famous People* by Wayne E. Warner. Grand Rapids: Baker Book House, 1972, p. 214.

[2]From *All About Angels* by A. S. Joppie. Grand Rapids: Baker Book House, 1953, p. 58.

[3]*The Greatest Is Love.* Wheaton, IL: Tyndale Foundation, copyright 1967.

[4]From *The Pulpit Commentary* by H. D. M. Spence and Joseph S. Exell. Chicago: Wilcox and Follett Co., Publishers, Vol. 34, p. 210.

[5]From *The Ministry of Angels* by C. S. Osterhus, D.D. Copyrighted. Osterhus Publishing House, 4500 W. Broadway, Minneapolis, MN 55422. Used by permission.

[6]From *Like a Mighty Wind* by Mel Tari. Copyright 1971 by Creation House. Used with permission.

[7]Roberta Teeter, personal interview, Sacramento, California, September 30, 1974.

[8]Mr. and Mrs. Ken Palmer, missionaries to the Ivory Coast of West Africa, letter to author, September 26, 1974.

[9]Glenda Rogers, missionary to the Republic of Zaire, letter to author, 1975.

Chapter 6

[1]Lois Shelton, missionary to Liberia, letter to author, August 29, 1974.

[2]Anna Stafsholt, missionary to Liberia, tape recording to author, November 4, 1974.

[3]*Ibid.*

Chapter 7

[1]*Sourcebook for Speakers* by Eleanor Doan. Grand Rapids: Zondervan Publishing House, 1968, p. 192.

[2]Louie Stokes, missionary to Argentina, letter to author, October 15, 1973.

[3]Reprinted from the *Pentecostal Evangel* by permission. Copyright 1973 by The General Council of the Assemblies of God.

Chapter 8

[1]From *The Ministry of Angels* by C. S. Osterhus. Copyrighted. Osterhus Publishing House, 4500 W. Broadway, Minneapolis, MN 55422. Used by permission.

[2]From *Heaven and Angels* by H. A. Baker. Published by Osterhus Publishing House, 4500 W. Broadway, Minneapolis, MN 55422. Used by permission. Pages 207, 208.

[3]From *Angels* by James Check. Published by Osterhus Publishing House, 4500 W. Broadway, Minneapolis, MN 55422. Used by permission.

Chapter 9

[1]From *Sourcebook for Speakers* by Eleanor Doan. Grand Rapids: Zondervan Publishing House, 1968, p. 261.

[2]Mrs. John J. Friesen, "Do You Know Christ Lives?" *The Evangel;* Official Voice of the International Assemblies of God, Roodepoort, Transvaal, South Africa; Vol. 3, No. 1 (March 1971), pp. 1, 3. Used by permission.

[3]From *The Great Doctrines of the Bible* by William Evans, Ph.D., D.D. Chicago: Moody Press, 1912, p. 219.

[4]Mr. and Mrs. Ken Palmer, missionaries to the Ivory Coast of West Africa, letter to author, September 26, 1974.

[5]Mark Buntain, missionary to Calcutta, India, letter to author, October 31, 1973.

[6]Walter E. Erickson, missionary to Lima, Peru, letter to author, December 15, 1973.

[7]B. T. Bard, missionary to Germany, letter to author, October 13, 1973.

Chapter 10

[1]Hymman O. Wood, missionary to Nigeria, letter to author, February 27, 1974.

[2]See *Introduction to Prophecy* by Frank M. Boyd. Springfield, MO: Gospel Publishing House, 1948, p. 19.